Lecture Notes in Business Information Processing **221**

Series Editors

Wil van der Aalst
Eindhoven Technical University, Eindhoven, The Netherlands
John Mylopoulos
University of Trento, Povo, Italy
Michael Rosemann
Queensland University of Technology, Brisbane, QLD, Australia
Michael J. Shaw
University of Illinois, Urbana-Champaign, IL, USA
Clemens Szyperski
Microsoft Research, Redmond, WA, USA

More information about this series at http://www.springer.com/series/7911

Isabelle Linden · Shaofeng Liu
Fátima Dargam · Jorge E. Hernández (Eds.)

Decision Support Systems IV – Information and Knowledge Management in Decision Processes

Euro Working Group Conferences, EWG-DSS 2014
Toulouse, France, June 10–13, 2014
and Barcelona, Spain, July 13–18, 2014
Revised Selected and Extended Papers

 Springer

Editors
Isabelle Linden
University of Namur
Namur
Belgium

Fátima Dargam
SimTech Simulation Technology
Graz
Austria

Shaofeng Liu
University of Plymouth
Plymouth
UK

Jorge E. Hernández
University of Liverpool
Liverpool
UK

ISSN 1865-1348   ISSN 1865-1356   (electronic)
Lecture Notes in Business Information Processing
ISBN 978-3-319-21535-8   ISBN 978-3-319-21536-5   (eBook)
DOI 10.1007/978-3-319-21536-5

Library of Congress Control Number: 2015943829

Springer Cham Heidelberg New York Dordrecht London

Printed on acid-free paper

Springer International Publishing AG Switzerland is part of Springer Science+Business Media
(www.springer.com)

Preface

This fourth edition of the EURO Working Group on Decision Support Systems (EWG-DSS) includes selected and extended papers from two major events organized by EWG-DSS in 2014, complemented by an open call on the topic "Information and Knowledge Management in Decision Processes." The events include the GDN 2014 conference, co-organized by the EWG-DSS and the INFORMS-GDN group; and the DSS Stream organized by the EWG-DSS in the IFORS international conference. Both events were partially supported and sponsored by the EURO Working Group on Decision Support Systems (EWG-DSS) and the Association of European Operational Research Societies (EURO), respectively, in cooperation with: the Business Administration Department of the University of Macedonia in Greece; SimTech Simulation Technology in Austria; University of Toulouse and the Institut de Research en Informatique de Toulouse (IRIT) in France; the University of Liverpool Management School (ULMS) in the UK; UNINOVA Computational Intelligence Research Group (CA3) in Portugal; School of Management, University of Plymouth in the UK; Instituto de Lógica Filosofia e Teoria da Ciência (ILTC) in Brazil; the University of Namur in Belgium; and the University of Belgrade in Serbia.

The major objective of both the GDN 2014 Conference held in Toulouse, France, during June 10–13, 2014, and the 20th IFORS International Conference – DSS Stream (with eight sessions) held in Barcelona, Spain, during July 13–18, 2014, was to bring together academics, researchers, practitioners, and enterprise professionals interested in modeling, implementing, and deploying decision support systems for enhancing the decision-making process in different types of environments, considering conceptual as well as applied approaches. Contributions in both events involved a rich variety of themes. Particular attention was focused on information and knowledge management in decision processes.

At the two events, over 120 papers were presented and assessed by a group of experts and reviewers, including members of the EWG-DSS. In conjunction with the two important events organized by EWG-DSS in 2014 and the open call, we assembled a collection of high-quality submissions. Ten papers of the highest quality as ranked by the Selection Committee were chosen and the authors were invited to extend their papers and submit them for consideration to the LNBIP publication. Moreover, the open Call for Papers attracted another four submissions. The submitted papers were then put through a rigorous review process. Finally, eight papers that received the best evaluation results from the reviewers were selected for publication in this book.

The selected contributions comprise a set of four papers focused on knowledge sharing: "The Contribution of Knowledge Sharing to Organizational Performance and Decision Making: A Literature Review," authored by Femi Olan, Shaofeng Liu, and Irina Neaga; "Multicriteria Decision Aid Method for Knowledge Sharing," authored by Sarra Bouzayane and Inès Saad; "A Collaborative Spatial Decision Support System for the Capacitated Vehicle Routing Problem on a Tabletop Display," authored by Nikolaos Ploskas, Ioannis Athanasiadis, Jason Papathanasiou, and Nikolaos Samaras; and the contribution entitled "Trust and Understanding in Face-to-Face and Online Negotiation," by Yvonne van der Toorn, Per van der Wijst, and Debby Damen.

A second set of four papers studies the information models developed to support the decision process: "Discovering Characteristics That Affect Process Control Flow," authored by Pavlos Delias, Daniela Grigori, Mohamed Lamine Mouhoub, and Alexis Tsoukias; "Study on Temporal Change of Social Context: In the Case of Bicycle Riding Issue in Japan," authored by Madoka Chosokabe, Hiroki Takeyoshi, and Hiroyuki Sakakibara; and the contribution entitled "Timing and Decision Making" by Gil Greenstein.

We would like to take this opportunity to express our gratitude to all those who contributed to the EWG-DSS research events in 2014, including authors, reviewers, Program Committees, and institutional sponsors. Finally, we hope you will find the contents of this EWG-DSS LNBIP edition useful and interesting for your own research activities.

July 2014

Isabelle Linden
Shaofeng Liu
Fátima Dargam
Jorge E. Hernández

EURO Working Group on Decision Support Systems

The EWG-DSS is a Working Group on Decision Support Systems within EURO, the Association of the European Operational Research Societies. The main purpose of the EWG-DSS is to establish a platform for encouraging state-of-the-art high-quality research and collaboration work within the DSS community. Other aims of the EWG-DSS are to:

- Encourage the exchange of information among practitioners, end-users, and researchers in the area of decision systems.
- Enforce networking among the DSS communities available and facilitate activities that are essential for the start up of international cooperation research and projects.
- Facilitate professional, academic, and industrial opportunities for its members.
- Favor the development of innovative models, methods, and tools in the field decision support and related areas.
- Actively promote the interest in decision systems in the scientific community by organizing dedicated workshops, seminars, mini-conferences, and conference streams in major conferences, as well as editing special and contributed issues in relevant scientific journals.

The EWG-DSS was founded with 24 members, during the EURO Summer Institute on DSS that took place at Madeira, Portugal, in May 1989, organized by two well-known academics of the OR community: Jean-Pierre Brans and José Paixão. The EWG-DSS group has substantially grown along the years. Currently, we have over 250 registered multinational members.

Through the years, much collaboration among the group members generated valuable contributions to the DSS field, which resulted in many journal publications. Since its creation, the EWG-DSS has held annual meetings in various European countries, and has taken active part in the EURO conferences on decision-making-related subjects. Starting from 2015, the EWG-DSS is establishing a new annually organized conference, namely, the International Conference on Decision Support System Technology (ICDSST).

The EWG-DSS Coordination Board comprises: Pascale Zaraté (France), Fátima Dargam (Austria), Rita Ribeiro (Portugal), Shaofeng Liu (UK), Isabelle Linden (Belgium), Jorge E. Hernández (UK/Chile), Jason Papathanasiou (Greece), and Boris Delibašić (Serbia).

Reviewing Committee

Adiel Teixeira De Almeida	Federal University of Pernambuco, Brazil
Francisco Antunes	INESC Coimbra and Beira Interior University, Portugal
Marko Bohanec	Jožef Stefan Institute, Slovenia
João Clímaco	University of Coimbra, Portugal

Contents

The Contribution of Knowledge Sharing to Organizational Performance and Decision Making: A Literature Review

Femi Olan[(✉)], Shaofeng Liu, and Irina Neaga

Graduate School of Management, Plymouth University, Plymouth, UK
femi.olan@northumbria.ac.uk,{shaofeng.liu,
irina.neaga}@plymouth.ac.uk

Abstract. In current knowledge economy, organizations have identified knowledge sharing as a catalyst to improve business. Therefore, the need to build relationships between organizational processes and knowledge activities are crucial to gain competitive advantages over competitors. However, there are new challenges facing organizations in transferring from business processes to knowledge processes. This paper suggests an integrative knowledge sharing performance framework based on the analysis of literature and the exploration of key performance indicators. Performance measurement is used to evaluate and measure the impact of knowledge sharing to organizational performance, this measurement can further provide support for organizational decision making. A major contribution of this paper is providing suggestions for future research and practices on how knowledge sharing can improve efficiency and effectiveness of employees, also reduce cost and errors in organizational business processes.

Keywords: Organizational decision making · Knowledge sharing · Performance measurement · Knowledge process

1 Introduction

The pattern of change of organizational capitalism has evolved in the last two decades, interest in knowledge management has grown significantly [1–4]. In the same vein, the contributions of related studies in knowledge management, performance management and decision support literature has increased exponentially [5–8], these contributions consist of concepts, applications and interaction of various paradigms of management. Knowledge is a key essential tool for organizational decision making [9–12]. Therefore, there is a swift change in capital investment from physical resources to intellectual resources. The knowledge economy has provided an enabling competitive environment where performance and profitability is driven by organizational owned knowledge apparatus. The need to introduce knowledge sharing concept to augment business processes across all sectors of the organization, which avail the edge above competitors in the industry [13]. However, the success of implementing knowledge sharing with the organizational business processes is dependent on essential organizational factors; these factors can be internal and/or external [14]. According to scholars in this field,

© Springer International Publishing Switzerland 2015
I. Linden et al. (Eds.): EWG-DSS 2014, LNBIP 221, pp. 1–12, 2015.
DOI: 10.1007/978-3-319-21536-5_1

knowledge sharing activities significantly contributed to improving performance, which will directly support decision making [15–17]. Management of decision support systems are influenced by the impacts of knowledge sharing activities on critical management tasks.

The aim of this paper is to provide an in-depth literature review on the knowledge sharing contribution to organizational performance and decision making. An integrative knowledge sharing performance (IKSP) framework has been developed to knit the literature into a body of knowledge and provide guidance to the analysis of literature, in order to elicit future directions. The IKSP can provide an overall picture of future directions in how to facilitate and enhance organizational performance for decision making through the identification of key performance indicators for the actual measurement of the contribution of knowledge sharing to organizational performance.

The sections of this paper are organized as follows. Section 2 introduces the IKSP framework used to analyze the literature. Major findings of the literature review and recommendations for future research are presented in Sect. 3. Finally, Sect. 4 draws conclusions.

2   Deriving an Integrated Knowledge Sharing Performance (IKSP) Framework

A large amount of existing research studies has been published relating to the topic in this review. The main purpose of this literature review is not just to provide a "shopping list" of the published work, but to provide an overview of the body of knowledge, and more importantly to elicit research gaps in the literature and suggest future research directions. Hence, it is important that a framework is developed in order to systematically knit the literature to reveal the relevance and trends of existing work. This section starts with the key components of the IKSP framework, including knowledge sharing, SECI model, Japanese Ba theory and performance measurement approaches.

2.1   SECI Model for Knowledge Sharing

In a knowledge driven environment, knowledge sharing is the platform where employees directly/indirectly mutually ex-change individual 'know-how', 'know-what' and 'know-why'. Based on Nonaka and Takeuchi [18], the Socialization, Externalization, Combination and Internalization (SECI) model introduced the knowledge creation process [19–22]. In categorizing the SECI model, internalization and socialization as knowledge sharing process converts organizational knowledge to individual knowledge, while combination and externalization as knowledge sharing process is the transfer of individual knowledge to organizational knowledge. Organizations deploy knowledge sharing activities as a means of tackling unresolved problems, innovation and cost reduction. However, implementation of successful knowledge sharing practices has benefits to organization, such as improved performance and decision making. Tacit and explicit knowledge are the foundations for socialization and combination respectively, while for externalization and internalization, it will be classified as an equal share of contribution by Abdulla and Mehairi, Akiyoshi, and Blackler [23–25].

2.2 Japanese Ba Theory for Knowledge Sharing

Japanese Ba theory has described by [26–29] relates social context environment with knowledge interaction. There are four types of Ba which are associated with SECI model; originating, dialoguing, systemizing and exercising Ba [30]. It is necessary to understand the characteristics of each Ba concept with SECI model, also the impact on organizational performance and decision making in general. The following sub-sections discuss the bonding of SECI model and Ba theory.

- Socialization/Originating Ba
  The social context of interaction is described as face-to-face and individuality. This is characterized by care, love, trust and commitment when individuals are sharing experiences, mental models, emotions and feelings. This social context is required when sharing tacit knowledge, also the difficulty in capturing tacit knowledge makes it obligatory to create environment empathy [31, 32]. There is continuity of knowledge transcending from one individual to another during interaction.

- Externalization/Dialoguing Ba
  The social context of interaction is described as face-to-face and collective, this is characterized by sharing personalized mental models and 'know-how', which is grouped as common class and are documented as verified concepts. Therefore, this is an environment where individuals' 'tacit' knowledge is captured during knowledge activities through the organization medium, such as problem solving capturing tools [28, 29]. Dialoguing Ba is conscience with the creation of new knowledge by developing efficient collaboration of individuals with specific tacit knowledge.

- Combination/Systemizing Ba
  The social context of interaction is described as collective and virtual, knowledge activities are characterized by the consolidation of existing explicit knowledge. It is easier to communicate explicit knowledge in this environment to a big number of individuals using documented resources. In addition, the role of information technology aids knowledge sharing through a collective virtual environment for transfer of explicit knowledge [29, 31]. Among the information technological tools used in combination/systemizing Ba are on-line network, databanks, groupware and social networks. In recent time, organizations promote knowledge sharing by introducing electronic mailing lists and online problem solving groups which consist of employees [28], this medium allows free sharing of collective knowledge to improve performance for making effective and efficient decisions.

- Internalization/Exercising Ba
  The social context of interaction is described as individual and virtual, knowledge activities are characterized with the conversion of explicit to tacit knowledge. Employees in the organization gain organizational knowledge which is available through virtual media, such as simulation programs and organizational learning

[32, 33]. Internalization/exercising Ba can be synthesized through continuous practice and action [27, 29].

2.3 Performance Measurement

Existing literature in performance draws from various fields of work, increasingly suggests that performance measurement is beneficial to most areas of management and decision making, a good example of the application of performance management is operations management [34]. However, there are research arguments in the performance field suggesting that performance management may not worth investing time and researching on, although literature exists on appropriate performance measurements and the identification of negative outcomes when inappropriate performance indicators are used for measurement [35–37]. Studies have shown that performance measurement is a tool which organizations use for assessment and evaluation of processes, this paper move to achieve the measurement of the contribution of knowledge sharing to improve organizational processes. Research in performance measurement also shows that carrying out test with different quantitative links yield conflicting result, which proves that there are different measuring indicators for a particular performance input. Emerging studies in this field check for comparable quantitative output for input with particular measures indicators [38].

2.4 The Integrative Knowledge Sharing Performance (IKSP) Framework

A large number of related articles have elaborately presented knowledge sharing and its benefits to organization in various capacities. However, there is little related work on the contribution of knowledge sharing to organizational performance in relation to decision making. Hence, the research gap as identified is to measure the contribution of knowledge sharing with specific KPIs 'key performance indicators' [39]. In the literature, the social context in which knowledge conversion takes place was extensively discussed and how knowledge participants play critical role. IKSP framework is a knowledge approach with two knowledge sharing categorizations; where the environment for interaction is considered to be face-to-face. Hence, the need to create an organizational culture based on trust, love, and shared mental model which reflects the vision of leadership. As shown in Fig. 1. There are three stages of communication;

- The initial stage for knowledge sharing is to identify employees with experiences which reflects the technical and business 'know-how', also the environment for knowledge interaction
- The performance stage is the measuring of the impact/contribution of knowledge with performance indicators, these indicators are industry specific i.e. an industry decides on the processes which indicators are measured with
- Lastly, the decision stage uses some analytical tools to draw conclusions on the efficiency of the knowledge transformation process.

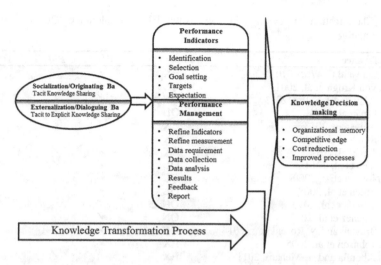

Fig. 1. Integrative knowledge sharing performance (IKSP) framework for decision making.

KPIs are set values or figures which are tools used to measure against targets, goals, and objectives. KPIs provide the platform to compare both internal and external targeted performance milestones. KPIs in IKSP framework are characterized by; (1) the lesser the number of indicators, the better the performance. (2) Knowledge impacted processes should be measured against real factors. (3) Comparing of indicators should reflect past, present, and future. (4) The interest of stakeholders should come first when designing indicators. (5) To achieve a more comprehensive performance, complex indicators should be simplified. KPIs represent organizational key success factors.

2.5 IKSP in Decision Support Systems

Comparatively little research has been conducted on the direct relationship between SECI Model and Japanese Ba theory. Tacit knowledge promises competitive advantage in the evolving organization knowledge decision processes and therefore the measurements of new knowledge processes using the concept of KPIs, provides alliance with decision support systems [40]. On the other hand, tacit knowledge is difficult to share and inherently hinders capitalizing in decision making. However, the need for more research to consolidate previous results and to further understanding of how knowledge characterized by different combinations of the aforementioned characteristics affects decision support processes.

Furthermore, research has examined knowledge sharing from a general standpoint impact on relatively global scales – the extent to which know-how or knowledge processes impact decision support systems [41–45]. A more precise survey of organizational knowledge assets as limited objects of decision making, allowing for more precise elaboration of the effects of knowledge characteristics on organizational decision processes (Table 1).

Table 1. Classification of review evidences. Note: EX = Explorative; QL = Qualitative; QN = Quantitative

Reference	Impact	KS	PM	DM
S. Liao and C. Wu, 2010	EX	✓		
G. von Krogh et al, 2001	QL	✓		
H. Alali and J. Salim, 2013	QN	✓		
C. Liu et al, 2014	QL		✓	
M. Birasnav, 2013	EX	✓	✓	
B. Reich et al, 2014	EX	✓	✓	✓
Y. Lai et al, 2014	EX	✓	✓	✓
T. Kim et al, 2014	QL	✓	✓	✓
I. Nonaka et al, 2000	QL	✓		
Z. Erden et al, 2008	QL	✓		
A. Pässila et al, 2013	QN	✓		✓
J. Sánchez et al, 2013.	QN	✓		
S. Brusoni and N. Rosenkranz, 2014	QN	✓		
G. Johnson et al, 2005	EX	✓		
H. Abdulla and A. Mehairi, 2011	EX		✓	
M. Akiyoshi, 2008	QL	✓		
F. Blackler, 1995	QL	✓		
M. Westerman, 2014	QN	✓	✓	✓
J. Young, 2012	QN	✓		
W. Hanks, 2014	QN	✓		
G. Jiang et al, 2014	QL	✓		
L. Shu et al, 2013	EX	✓		✓
M. Lyles, 2014	EX	✓		✓
R. Maruta, 2014	EX	✓		
D. Esterhuizen et al, 2012	EX	✓		✓
J. Hao et al, 2014	EX	✓	✓	
P. Coram et al, 2011	EX		✓	
G. Castro et al, 2008	EX		✓	
Y. Senoo, and R. Watanabe, 2010	EX	✓		
T. Sumita et al, 2009	QL	✓		
I. Nonaka et al, 2014	QL	✓		✓
I. Nonaka et al, 2002	QN	✓		
T. Alolah, 2014	QL		✓	
H. Wu, 2012	QN		✓	
S. Toor and S. Ogunlana, 2010	EX		✓	
M. Lahoz and J. Camarotto, 2012	EX		✓	
A. Draghici, 2014	EX		✓	
A. Enoma and S. Allen, 2007	QL		✓	
Y. Tsai and Y. Cheng, 2012	QN		✓	✓
C. Ivanov and S. Avasilc i, 2014	QN		✓	✓
S. Liu et al, 2015	QN	✓		✓
R. Speklé and F. Verbeeten, 2014	QN		✓	
K. Howell and F. Annansingh, 2013	EX	✓		
A. Alkhuraiji et al, 2014	EX	✓		✓
U. Jayawickrama et al, 2013	EX	✓		✓
B. Wier et al, 2007	EX		✓	
S. Baños-Caballero et al, 2014	QL		✓	
A. Abdel-Maksoud et al, 2005	QL		✓	
S. Liu, 2014	QN	✓		✓
E. Neaga and J. Harding, 2005	QN	✓		

In conclusion, supporting decision making, key knowledge indicators measure the performance of knowledge sharing by comparing the outcome of the organizational process before the implementation of knowledge sharing and after. IKSP framework is a continuous knowledge management framework which is designed to integrate knowledge sharing actively with organizational activities to achieve optimal performance.

3 Major Findings and Future Research Directions

This section discusses major findings and future research directions using the IKSP framework for the analysis of literature, with a focus on how knowledge sharing contributes to organizational decision support. The findings and future directions are organized around, two critical features: Knowledge sharing features and performance measurement features and decision Support Systems and its relationship with knowledge management and information sharing in organization.

3.1 Knowledge Sharing Features

With the identification of research gap from literature, it is important to consider main limitations to the integration of knowledge sharing with organizational processes. The role of knowledge sharing for future research needs to support decision making through its impact on performance. Therefore, the foundation of knowledge has to be embedded in the processes of the organization, starting with the types of knowledge, tacit knowledge as a type of knowledge is context specific, therefore it is very difficult to document, codify and communicate [46]. However, tacit knowledge is understood to be the hub where new knowledge initiate. On the other hand, explicit knowledge is knowledge which can be codify, documented and easily communicated. Hence, the transfer of explicit knowledge is easier carried out through a channel while tacit knowledge requires enabling environment for transfer [11], the difficulties in measuring 'know-what', 'know-why', and 'know-how' have limited related literature [47, 48]. Knowledge sharing strategy ensures that organizations are capable of developing organizational memory by integrating existing knowledge from employees' knowledge domains. Ultimately, considering the fact that organizational memory is built on experiences of employees which are gained over a period of time, therefore the interaction of employees with organizational processes over time deposits new knowledge which improves performance. This feature sets out the knowledge domains which is in existence and focus on sharing that knowledge from individuals to groups, from groups to departments and from departments to the entire organization as a whole. In terms of strategic decision support, the contribution of knowledge sharing is an orientation towards attaining efficiency in organizational processes as well as improving competitive advantage. Knowledge sharing strategy ensures that organizations are capable of developing organizational memory by integrating existing knowledge from employees' knowledge domains.

3.2 Performance Measurement Features

Organizational performance [49] is classified into three main levels; financial, non-financial, and operational level. The financial level of an organizational performance is the net profit derived after sales. Almost all companies focus more on finance performance [39–42]. The non-financial level is considered as the employees' satisfaction, the outcome of finance performance most often dependent on the non-financial performance, while operational level is the performance of the market share, quality of products and services [24]. However, financial and operational performance is directly influence by the efficiency of non-financial performance [25]. During the last two decades, there is a shift from measuring only financial performance to financial and non-financial performance of assets and liabilities. The annual report of the organization reflects the cordial relationship between financial and non-financial entities.

Performance measurement provide a comprehensive view of the organization's achievement over a given period of time, this achievement varies when comparing time periods, and performance is subjected to factors such as; government policy, environmental conditions and other external influences [16, 17]. Therefore, the contribution of either hampers the performance of the other. Most financial performance measurements have national and international report standards. There are guide-lines which are supervised by financial governing institutions, hence, the measurement of financial performance of the organization is easy to quantify. On the other hand, there exist little or no non-financial governing institutions to design a uniform measuring guide-line for the organizations.

In future research, the measurement of knowledge sharing activities needs to be implemented using key knowledge performance indicators, these indicators can be also known as success factors. Knowledge sharing activities are measured using knowledge specific indicators; these indicators are context-defined data collections from organizational processes which interact with knowledge sharing activities.

3.3 Decision Support Systems and Its Relationship with Knowledge Management and Information Sharing in Organization

In this paper, IKSP framework emphasized on identifying and integrating resourceful know-how for organizational decision processes. Two knowledge fundamentals, i.e. SECI model and Japanese Ba theory produced an inter-relationship between the organizational knowledge holders and the context-defined environment which has been specified [6–9]. The advancements realized in organizational knowledge decision processes can be theorized based on contributions stressed in the literature on knowledge and performance issues within the organization. In addition, the introduction of context knowledge application to organization processes provides leverage for interaction between knowledge holders; consequently, reducing operations turnaround time and processes, supporting organizational decision processes. A key benefit of discovering knowledge processes for IKSP is that it propagates expansion of 'organization memory' for the success of organizational operations through advanced 'time-to-decision' [21–24]. Eventually, the knowledge processes and the measurement

Table 2. Summary of research findings.

Research unit of analysis	Findings	Research gaps
Subject specifics	Broad range of different theories and models	Lack of research with continuous approach for dynamic processes
	More quantitative approach	
Knowledge sharing processes	Approaches concentrate more finding on theories	Lack of research on KSP application
Knowledge performance measurement	Broad research arguments findings on performance measurement	Lack of research on integration of knowledge processes with performance measurement
Organizational knowledge processes	Little research arguments available	Inadequate research on the subject

of the contribution to organizational decision processes model can resourcefully support the collaborative decision-making between various knowledge entities, precisely, in transiting from organizational processes to organization knowledge processes. Considering the leadership implication, the benefits of IKSP includes making justifiable integrated decisions based on sufficient planning, sourcing and valuation provided from measureable performance objectives [31–34] (Table 2).

4   Conclusions

This paper reviews existing work focused on contribution of knowledge sharing to organizational performance, and organizational support decision making. An integrated knowledge sharing performance (IKSP) framework has been defined to analyze the literature. Three major landmarks are significantly instrumental in the contextual lay-out of this paper, i.e. the SECI model, Ba theory and Performance measurement. The interaction between SECI model and Ba theory has been specified for future research. Focusing on the outcomes of the literature review, priority should be given to measuring knowledge sharing processes which have added more values to organizational processes and also provide support for decision making [39, 40].

The limitations of this paper are as follows: (1) there are organizational factors which can hinder the successful implementation of IKSP framework, but these factors can be managed based on the interest of the leadership structure. (2) The availability data for empirical analysis is also constricting factor.

This review paper is important for future research due to the following reasons: (1) An IKSP framework that can provide knowledge support for decision making in organizations, knowledge sharing can significantly improve organizational performance by providing an environment for knowledge innovation and support for employees through enumeration. (2) It provides guidance for the measurement of the output of organizational knowledge processes to equip organizations with cutting edge competitive advantage over competition. (3) It provides guidance based on literature review for the transition from organizational processes to knowledge processes which can reduce operations turnaround time and cost.

References

1. Alavi, M., Leidner, D.E.: Review knowledge management and knowledge management systems: conceptual foundations and research issues. MIS Q. **25**(1), 107–136 (2001)
2. Liao, S.H.: Knowledge management technologies and applications literature review from 1995 to 2002. Expert Syst. Appl. **25**(2), 155–164 (2003)
3. Yang, T.M., Maxwell, T.A.: Information-sharing in public organizations: a literature review of interpersonal, intra-organizational and inter-organizational success factors. Gov. Inf. Q. **28**(2), 164–175 (2011)
4. Maier, R., Hädrich, T.: Knowledge management systems. In: Schwartz, D., Teeni, D. (eds.) Encyclopedia of Knowledge Management. Information Science Reference, Hershey (2011)
5. Lee, M.R., Lan, Y.C.: Toward a unified knowledge management model for SMEs. Expert Syst. Appl. **38**(1), 729–735 (2011)
6. Hernández, J.E., Lyons, A.C., Poler, R., Mula, J., Goncalves, R.: A reference architecture for the collaborative planning modelling process in multi-tier supply chain networks: a zachman-based approach. Prod. Plann. Control **25**, 1–17 (2013)
7. Hernández, J.E., Alemany, M.M.E., Lario, F.C., Poler, R.: A supply chain agent-based modelling methodology that supports a collaborative planning process. Innova. **19**(34), 99–120 (2009)
8. Mula, J., Poler, R., Garcia-Sabater, J.P., Lario, F.C.: Models for production planning under uncertainty: a review. Int. J. Prod. Econ. **103**(1), 271–285 (2006)
9. Mula, J., Peidro, D., Díaz-Madroñero, M., Vicens, E.: Mathematical programming models for supply chain production and transport planning. Eur. J. Oper. Res. **204**(3), 377–390 (2010)
10. Krogh, G.V., Geilinger, N.: Knowledge creation in the eco-system: research imperatives. Eur. Manage. J. **32**(1), 155–163 (2014)
11. Liao, S.H., Wu, C.: System perspective of knowledge management, organizational learning, and organizational innovation. Expert Syst. Appl. **37**(2), 1096–1103 (2010)
12. Alali, H., Salim, J.: Virtual communities of practice success model to support knowledge sharing behaviour in healthcare sector. Procedia Technol. **11**(1), 176–183 (2013)
13. Liu, C., Wang, J., Li, H., Xue, Z., Deng, B., Wei, X.: Model-based iterative learning control of parkinsonian state in thalamic relay neuron. Commun. Nonlinear Sci Numer Simul. **19**(9), 3255–3266 (2014)
14. Alkhuraiji, A., Liu, S., Oderanti, F.O., Annansingh, F., Pan, J.: Knowledge network modelling to support decision-making for strategic intervention in IT project-oriented change management. J. Decis. Syst. **23**, 1–18 (2014)
15. Neaga, E.I., Harding, J.A.: An enterprise modeling and integration framework based on knowledge discovery and data mining. Int. J. Prod. Res. **43**(6), 1089–1108 (2005)
16. Howell, K.E., Annansingh, F.: Knowledge generation and sharing in UK universities: A tale of two cultures. Int. J. Inf. Manage. **33**(1), 32–39 (2013)
17. Nonaka, I., Toyama, R., Konno, N.: SECI, Ba and leadership: a unified model of dynamic knowledge creation. Long Range Plan. **33**(1), 5–34 (2000)

18. Erden, Z., Krogh, G.V., Nonaka, I.: The quality of group tacit knowledge. J. Strateg. Inf. Syst. **17**(1), 4–18 (2008)
19. Pässilä, A., Uotila, T., Melkas, H.: Facilitating future-oriented collaborative knowledge creation by using artistic organizational innovation methods: experiences from a finnish wood-processing company. Futures **47**, 59–68 (2013)
20. Sánchez, J.H., Sánchez, Y.H., Collado-Ruiz, D., Cebrián-Tarrasón, D.: Knowledge creating and sharing corporate culture framework. Procedia Soc. Behav. Sci. **74**, 388–397 (2013)
21. Brusoni, S., Rosenkranz, N.A.: Reading between the lines: Learning as a process between organizational context and individuals' proclivities. Eur. Manage. J. **32**(1), 147–154 (2014)
22. Abdulla, H., Mehairi, A.: Cultural influences on knowledge sharing behaviours through open system vs closed system cultures: the impact of organisational culture on knowledge sharing. no. 2009, pp. 475–482 (2011)
23. Akiyoshi, M.: Knowledge sharing over the network. Thin Solid Films **517**(4), 1512–1514 (2008)
24. Blackler, F.: Knowledge, knowledge work and organizations an overview and interpretation. Organ. Stud. **16**(6), 1021–1046 (1995)
25. Westerman, M.A.: Examining arguments against quantitative research: case studies illustrating the challenge of finding a sound philosophical basis for a human sciences approach to psychology. New Ideas Psychol. **32**, 42–58 (2014)
26. Hao, J., Yan, Y., Gong, L., Wang, G., Lin, J.: Knowledge map-based method for domain knowledge browsing. Decis. Support Syst. **61**, 106–114 (2014)
27. Coram, P.J., Mock, T.J., Monroe, G.S.: Financial analysts' evaluation of enhanced disclosure of non-financial performance indicators. Brit. Acc. Rev. **43**(2), 87–101 (2011)
28. Martín-de-Castro, G., López-Sáez, P., Navas-López, J.E.: Processes of knowledge creation in knowledge-intensive firms: Empirical evidence from Boston's Route 128 and Spain. Technovation **28**(4), 222–230 (2008)
29. Wu, Y., Senoo, D., Magnier-Watanabe, R.: Diagnosis for organizational knowledge creation: An ontological shift SECI model. J. Knowl. Manage. **14**(6), 791–810 (2010)
30. Sumita, T., Shimazaki, M., Matsuyama, K.: A proposal for inventory adjustment using multiple-layers SEC–CIS model. Int. J. Prod. Econ. **118**(1), 208–216 (2009)
31. Nonaka, I., Kodama, M., Hirose, A., Kohlbacher, F.: Dynamic fractal organizations for promoting knowledge-based transformation: a new paradigm for organizational theory. Eur. Manage. J. **32**(1), 137–146 (2014)
32. Nonaka, I., Sasaki, K., Ahmed, M.: The International Handbook on Innovation, pp. 882–889. Elsevier, Oxford (2003)
33. Wu, H.-Y.: Constructing a strategy map for banking institutions with key performance indicators of the balanced scorecard. Eval. Prog. Plann. **35**(3), 303–320 (2012)
34. Toor, S.-R., Ogunlana, S.O.: Beyond the iron triangle: stakeholder perception of key performance indicators for large-scale public sector development projects. Int. J. Pro.t Manage. **28**(3), 228–236 (2010)
35. Lahoz, M.D., Camarotto, J.A.: Performance indicators of work activity. Work **41**, 524–531 (2012)
36. Draghici, A., Popescu, A.-D., Gogan, L.M.: A proposed model for monitoring organizational performance. Procedia Soc. Behav. Sci. **124**, 544–551 (2014)
37. Ivanov, C.-I., Avasilcăi, S.: Performance measurement models: an analysis for measuring innovation processes performance. Procedia Soc. Behav. Sci. **124**, 397–404 (2014)
38. Tsai, Y.-C., Cheng, Y.-T.: Analyzing key performance indicators for E-commerce and internet marketing of elderly products: a review. Arch. Gerontol. Geriatr. **55**(1), 126–132 (2012)

39. Liu, S., Moizer, J., Megicks, P., Kasturiratne, D., Jayawickrama, U.: A knowledge chain management framework to support integrated decisions in global supply chains. Prod. Plann. Control **25**(8), 639–649 (2014)
40. Liu, S., Smith, M.H., Tuck, S., Pan, J., Alkuraiji, A., Jayawickrama, U.: Where can knowledge-based decision support systems go in contemporary business management: a new architecture for the future. J. Econ. Bus. Manage. **3**(5), 498–504 (2015)
41. Jayawickrama, U., Liu, S., Hudson Smith, M.: An integrative knowledge management framework to support erp implementation for improved management decision making in industry. In: Hernández, J.E., Liu, S., Delibašić, B., Zaraté, P., Dargam, F., Ribeiro, R. (eds.) EWG-DSS 2012. LNBIP, vol. 164, pp. 86–101. Springer, Heidelberg (2013)
42. Reich, B.H., Gemino, A., Sauer, C.: How knowledge management impacts performance in projects: An empirical study. Int. J. Project Manage. **32**(4), 590–602 (2014)
43. Lai, Y.-L., Hsu, M.-S., Lin, F.-J., Chen, Y.-M., Lin, Y.-H.: The effects of industry cluster knowledge management on innovation performance. J. Bus. Res. **67**(5), 734–739 (2014)
44. Kim, T.H., Lee, J.-N., Chun, J.U., Benbasat, I.: Understanding the effect of knowledge management strategies on knowledge management performance: A contingency perspective. Inf. Manage. **51**(4), 398–416 (2014)
45. Wier, B., Hunton, J., HassabElnaby, H.R.: Enterprise resource planning systems and non-financial performance incentives: The joint impact on corporate performance. Int. J. Acc. Inf. Syst. **8**(3), 165–190 (2007)
46. Birasnav, M.: Knowledge management and organizational performance in the service industry: the role of transformational leadership beyond the effects of transactional leadership. J. Bus. Res. **67**(8), 1622–1629 (2013)
47. Enoma, A., Allen, S.: Developing key performance indicators for airport safety and security. Facil. **25**(7/8), 296–315 (2007)
48. Speklé, R.F., Verbeeten, F.H.: The use of performance measurement systems in the public sector: effects on performance. Manage. Acc. Res. **25**(2), 131–146 (2014)
49. Johnson, G., Scholes, K., Whittington, R.: Exploring Corporate Strategy, vol. 8. Prentice Hall, London (2005)

Multicriteria Decision Aid Method for Knowledge Sharing

Sarra Bouzayane[1,2](✉) and Inès Saad[1,3]

[1] MIS Laboratory, University of Picardie Jules Verne,
33 Rue Saint Leu, 80039 Amiens, France
sarra.bouzayane@u-picardie.fr
http://home.mis.u-picardie.fr/~sarra/
[2] MIRACL Laboratory, Institute of Computer Science and Multimedia,
Route de Tunis Km, 10 B.P. 242, 3021 Sfax, Tunisia
[3] France Business School, Amiens, France

Abstract. In a delicate field such as the medical one, the decision-making process is extremely important given the major impact it can have on the patient's life. Indeed, the dramatic effects that can cause an inadequate decision make it primordial to strengthen the knowledge on which this decision is based. Thus, sharing knowledge between the members of the medical staff turns out to be a promising alternative to fulfill our goal consisting in enriching the medical background of the medical staff members in order to enable them to make a conscientious decision. Hence, this work develops a theoretical method representing a recommendation system relying on a Multicriteria Decision Aid method as well as on filtering techniques such as the collaborative filtering and the knowledge-based filtering aiming at improving the tacit and explicit knowledge sharing within organizations.

Keywords: Knowledge sharing · Collaborative filtering · Knowledge-based filtering · DRSA

1 Introduction

In some domains, namely the medical one, it is very important to share and to seamlessly disseminate the set of knowledge either preserved within an organization memory or embodied in the staff medical's minds in order to enrich their individual and collective background. Such exchange process helps professionals make the right decisions in complex clinical circumstances. Thus, this paper aims to better the problem of "knowledge sharing" within organizations, and particularly within the Association of Protection of Motors Disabled of Sfax-Tunisia (APMDS). This association is characterized by a large number of stakeholders with various profiles and different natures (internal or external ones, permanents or trainers, volunteers or salaried...) and who are usually geographically dispersed, which leads to problems in knowledge transmission between them. In addition, the absence of such an interaction between the stakeholders stops the

© Springer International Publishing Switzerland 2015
I. Linden et al. (Eds.): EWG-DSS 2014, LNBIP 221, pp. 13–25, 2015.
DOI: 10.1007/978-3-319-21536-5_2

knowledge development and limits it to the mind of each member. In fact, the knowledge within the APMDS is -always- at risk to be captured in the minds of its owners or therefore to be lost with their departure.

To overcome such a problem, this paper provides a theoretical method that targets the sharing of explicit knowledge preserved within an organizational memory and -also- the set of crucial but hardly explainable knowledge embodied in the human stakeholders' minds, called "tacit knowledge". This method is based on a recommendation system relying on a multicriteria decision aid approach and used as a sharing tool to provide the appropriate knowledge to a user needs. It plays the role of an intermediary between a transmitter who updates the system by the knowledge he possesses, and the receiver who accesses the system to seek knowledge that he needs. Yet, the knowledge sharing between the transmitter and the receiver does not require their physical presence. The method we propose relies mainly on the collaborative filtering technique based on DRSA (Dominance-based Rough Sets Approach) aiming at determining a set of users having tastes similar to the current user, called neighborhood. *A current user is the one for whom the recommendation system must provide an ordered list of knowledge meeting the needs he articulated in his query.* Moreover, to take into account the current user preferences, we have used the knowledge-based filtering technique to compare the current user query to the profile of knowledge already appreciated by his neighborhood. This study proposes reliable criteria to make multicriteria decisions about the knowledge "cruciality". Our aim, hence, is to help the medical staff members get the "appropriate" knowledge on the basis of which they can make the right decision.

This paper is organized as follows. Section two presents the background. Section three details our contribution. Section four illustrates the method by an example. Section five concludes the paper and underlines some future work.

2   Background

In this section, we present the DRSA method, the recommendation system and the knowledge sharing: Three concepts on which we have based our work.

2.1   Dominance-Based Rough Set Approach (DRSA)

DRSA method (Dominance-based Rough Set Approach) -developed by Greco [9]- is dedicated to the sorting problem in a *multicriteria decision aid* context. This is an extension of the rough sets theory to classify the reference actions within decision classes. This method allows the simultaneous consideration of criteria as well as of qualitative and quantitative attributes. The comparison of the actions is based on the dominance relation. Previous research has proposed the DRSA [9] to overcome the shortcomings of conventional rough sets theory [10] on multicriteria classification. The basic idea of DRSA is to replace the indiscernibility relation used in classical rough sets theory with the dominance relation, which is more appropriate for multicriteria decision-making. Moreover, unlike the probability theory [12] and the fuzzy set theory [6] where the inclusion of inconsistency requires the determination of probabilities or membership degrees, the DRSA method requires no additional information about data, which prompted us to use it. According to the method DRSA, a data table is a 4-tuple $S = \langle K, F, V, f \rangle$, where K is a finite set of reference actions, F is a finite set of criteria, $V = \cup_{g \in F} V_g$ is the set of possible values of criteria and f denote information function $f : F \times K \longrightarrow V$ such that $f(x, g) \in V_g, \forall x \in K, \forall g \in F$.

The criteria set F is divided into a set C of condition attributes and a decision attribute d. In a multicriteria classification, condition attributes are criteria. Furthermore, the decision attribute d makes a partition of K into a finite number of classes $Cl = \{Cl_t; t \in T\}$, $T = \{1..n\}$. Each $x \in K$ belongs to one and only one class $Cl_t \in Cl$. The classes from Cl are in a preference order following the increasing order of class indices, i.e. for all $r, s \in T$, such that $r > s$, the objects from Cl_r are preferred to the objects from Cl_s. Thus, the sets to be approximated are not particular classes but upward and downward unions of classes, thus:

$$Cl_t^{\leq} = \cup_{s \leq t} Cl_s, Cl_t^{\geq} = \cup_{s \geq t} Cl_s; t = 1...n$$

Definition 1. *(Dominance relation) Let $P \subseteq F$ be a subset of criteria. The dominance relation D_P associated with P is defined as follow:*

$$\forall(x, y) \in K, x D_P y \Leftrightarrow f(x, g_j) \succeq f(y, g_j) \forall g_j \in P$$

With each object $x \in K$, are associated:

- *a set of objects dominating x, called P-dominating set, $D_P^+(x) = \{y \in K : y D_P x\}$ and;*
- *a set of objects dominated by x, called P-dominated set, $D_P^-(x) = \{y \in K : x D_P y\}$.*

Definition 2. *(Lower approximation) Lower approximation of unions of classes represents a certain knowledge provided by criteria $P \subseteq F$.*

- *$\underline{P}(Cl_t^{\geq}) = \{ x \in K : D_P^+(x) \subseteq Cl_t^{\geq}, \forall t = 1...n \}$: the set of all objects belonging to $Cl_t^{\geq}$ without any ambiguity. It contains all objects whose P-dominating set is assigned with certainty to classes that are at least as good as Cl_t.*
- *$\underline{P}(Cl_t^{\leq}) = \{ x \in K : D_P^-(x) \subseteq Cl_t^{\leq}, \forall t = 1...n \}$: the set of all objects belonging to $Cl_t^{\leq}$ without any ambiguity. It contains all objects whose P-dominated set is assigned with certainty to classes that are at most as good as Cl_t.*

Definition 3. *(Boundary) We call boundary of Cl_t the set of actions which are uncertainly classified in the decision class Cl_t. It is represented as follow:*

- *$Bn_p(Cl_t^{\geq}) = \bar{P}(Cl_t^{\geq}) - \underline{P}(Cl_t^{\geq})$: set of all objects belonging to $Cl_t^{\geq}$ with some ambiguity.*
- *$Bn_p(Cl_t^{\leq}) = \bar{P}(Cl_t^{\leq}) - \underline{P}(Cl_t^{\leq})$: set of all objects belonging to $Cl_t^{\leq}$ with some ambiguity.*

Definition 4. *(Quality of approximation) It is the quality of classification performed by a decision maker for a giver decision class with respect to the set of criteria $P \subseteq F$. It is defined as the ratio between the number of P-correctly classified objects and the number of all the objects in the data sample set. It can be written as:*

$$\gamma_P = \frac{|K - (\cup_{t=1...n} Bn_p(Cl_t^{\leq})) \cup (\cup_{t=1...n} Bn_p(Cl_t^{\geq}))|}{|K|}$$

Definition 5. *(Core) For a given set of decision examples, it is possible to determine which criteria are relevant for the approximation of the attribution made by the decision maker agent. We call such subsets of relevant criteria, the "reducts" and we call their intersection, the "Core". Otherwise, for each minimal subset of criteria $P \subseteq F$ such as γ_P (Cl)= γ_F (Cl), P is called a reduct of F. A decision table can contain several reducts and their intersection set is the "Core".*

The DRSA method deals with the problem of the decision maker hesitation when assigning knowledge within a decision class which produces an uncertain assignment. In fact, DRSA method distinguishes between two sets of assignment: the certain assignments which represent the "Lower approximation" and the uncertain or ambiguous ones that represent the "Boundary". Thus, knowing his boundary, a decision-maker has always the possibility of revising his uncertain assignments in order to clear his Boundary and make the right decisions.

The concepts defined by the DRSA method will be used as inputs and outputs to develop the filtering techniques of the recommendation system in order to ensure knowledge sharing between the different system's users.

2.2 Recommendation System

According to [3], the recommendation system *is a software tool that has the effect of guiding users in a personalized way to interesting or useful objects in a large space of possible options.* In literature, several filtering techniques have been proposed to define a recommendation system, namely the collaborative filtering [8], the hybrid filtering [3], the knowledge-based filtering [4], etc. In our medical context, as we search the diversity and the novelty of knowledge, we have chosen the "collaborative filtering technique" [8] to take into account the opinions of all the users. We have also used the "knowledge-based filtering" [4] as a way of comparing the user query with the knowledge profile.

– *Collaborative Filtering* [8]: It is one of the earliest and most promising recommendation techniques. It provides recommendations by applying the matching principle that puts together users with similar interests. This filtering technique predicts items that can be appreciated by the current user, on the basis of opinions (ratings) expressed by other people for the same items. It defines a neighborhood for each user: it is the set of users who "liked" items that have already been appreciated by the current user. It takes as input the user's profile and the data on the community. It -then- applies a similarity function to determine the neighborhood so as to provide a list of recommendations.

– *Knowledge-based Filtering* [4]: It applies inferences on a set of items to find a particular one that must meet a specific need of a current user. This technique takes as input the user profile and the characteristics of all items. The conversational process of knowledge based recommendation always respects the following steps: the current user starts by specifying his requirements. Then, the system compares these requirements with the characteristics of the existing items to find those that meet the current user's requirements. Finally, the system will recommend an ordered list of the resulting items.

2.3 Knowledge Sharing

According to [5], *knowledge sharing is both a process of transmission and of absorption (use)*. In literature, many studies have focused on the issue of knowledge sharing within organizations. Some of them proposed theoretical models that bring a conceptual framework for several knowledge sharing processes where the most popular are the SECI model [11] and the BOISOT I-space KM model [2].

SECI Model [11]: The SECI (Socialization, Externalization, Combination, Internalization) model focuses on the creation and the transformation of knowledge. Organizations create and use knowledge through series of conversions:

– Socialization: the transformation from a tacit knowledge related to only one person to a set of tacit knowledge related to a group of people.
– Externalization: the transformation of tacit knowledge to an explicit one among individuals within a group. It requires a structuring effort to express tacit knowledge in a comprehensive form for the others.
– Combination: the process of creating new forms of explicit knowledge from the existing one.
– Internalization: the process of understanding and absorbing explicit knowledge into tacit knowledge held by the individual.

The SECI model describes the conversion of knowledge into a dynamic mode. It is based on the transformation of the tacit knowledge into an explicit one.

BOISOT I-Space KM Model [2]: In Boisot's scheme, knowledge assets can be located within a dimensional space defined by three axes: from "uncodified" to "codified", from "concrete" to "abstract" and from "undiffused" to "diffused". Thus, knowledge is structured, understood and shared via three steps:

– Codification: The process of transformation of knowledge into a tangible and an explicit form (code, documents...) in order to be communicated more widely and at a low cost.
– Abstraction: Recently codified knowledge is more adapted to the context in which it is applied.
– Diffusion: New knowledge is shared with a target population in a codified and an abstract form.

Despite the importance of the knowledge sharing process, authors are limited to propose theoretical models without provide automated tools.

3   Recommendation System Based DRSA to Support the Organizational Knowledge Sharing

The aim of the APMDS (Association of Protection of Motors Disabled of Sfax-Tunisia) is to make an early medical management of children with cerebral palsy. It consists of *improving the monitoring and the evaluation of the early support of young children with cerebral palsy*. So, this care process is made by a succession of several actions in the form of medical and paramedical monitoring as well as of early assessment of these children. For each child, this care process takes as input a maximum of medical knowledge and generates a new set of knowledge that should be explained for other care processes. This new knowledge will be either preserved in documents or embodied in the minds of these stakeholders. However, due to the fact that stakeholders are often busy or geographically dispersed, the transmission of such knowledge is missing which prevents its reuse. Thus, our objective is to enhance the knowledge sharing process in order to prevent its loss and -so- to enrich the background of the medical staff.

In this section we present the main axes on which our recommendation system is based. First, we define a theoretical set of criteria to be used as inputs for the DRSA approach. Then, we introduce our knowledge sharing method.

3.1   Knowledge Evaluation Criteria

In order to identify a meaningful set of evaluation criteria, we have conducted a literary review. In our proposed method, these criteria will be applied as inputs to the DRSA method. Seven theoretical criteria have been identified:

- $g_1=$ Accessibility [11]: Denotes the extent to which knowledge is available, or easily and quickly retrievable.
- $g_2=$ Specificity [11]: Denotes the degree to which knowledge is dependent on many different contexts of use.
- $g_3=$ Codifiability [11]: Denotes the degree to which knowledge could be articulated in documents and software.
- $g_4=$ Timeliness [15]: Denotes how far knowledge is sufficiently up-to-date. It can be related to the time when knowledge is created, stored and accessed.
- $g_5=$ Completeness [15]: Denotes the extent to which knowledge is not missing and is of sufficient breadth and depth for the task at hand.
- $g_6=$ Relevancy [15]: Denotes the extent to which knowledge is applicable.
- $g_7=$ Accuracy [14]: Denotes how correct and error-free knowledge is.

To develop our method, we should validate these criteria using the constructive approach of Belton and Pictet [1]. In fact, successive meetings with the APMDS experts, each one separately, have to be organized. Each meeting shall be equipped with this theoretical criteria list and each expert can accept it without any modification, delete some criteria or add some others that do not exist but that he considers relevant. After each meeting this list will be updated. The meetings will be made in an iterative manner with all the decision makers (APMDSs experts) until reaching a collaborative list that satisfies all of them.

Preferences Table: According to DRSA [9], each knowledge $K_i \in K$ must to be evaluated on the basis of each criterion $g_j \in F$. The set of all identified knowledge, all identified criteria and all evaluations has to be collected in a matrix called *Preferences table* (see Fig. 1). This table is fulfilled by a "man study" and domain experts after a thorough study on the field. It is *common* to all decision-makers supposed to use the system.

To clarify the concepts of criterion and evaluation, we cite the example of the criterion g_1 that describes the knowledge accessibility level and that is already validated on our application field (APMDS). The evaluations of a knowledge K_i on the criterion g_1 can have three values which are: $V_{i,1}= 1=$ easy, $2 =$ medium, $3 =$ difficult. Thus, the value $f(K_1, g_1)= V_{1,1} =1$ means that the knowledge K_1 is easily accessible. To explain the concepts of tacit (K_1) and explicit (K_2) medical knowledge we give a reduced set of validated knowledge:

- $K_1=$ Experiential expertise on the research of abnormal movements;
- $K_2=$ Prescriptive knowledge on the assessment of intellectual level.

Based on this common preferences tables, each decision maker must build its own *decision table*.

Decision Table: In this work, two decision classes are identified: the class Cl_1 containing knowledge classified as "not crucial" and the class Cl_2 containing the one classified as "Crucial". We note *that knowledge is classified as crucial if it is relevant and necessary to solve problems related to a given objective of the organization.* Each decision maker has to classify the set of knowledge and so-to complete the column D by "1" if knowledge is not crucial and by "2" if it is (See Fig. 1). By adding the column D to the preferences table, the latter will be called a *decision table* that concerns a *specific* decision maker (see Fig. 1). Each decision maker has two possibilities to complete his column D: he can classify knowledge either on the basis of the preferences table or without considering theses evaluations but - only- according to his experience.

DRSA Application: In this paper we developed a Java program to run DRSA method. This program takes as input the decision table of a unique decision maker. In the preferences table, we have fixed a sample of thirty-four knowledge, called references knowledge. The "Calculate" button (see Fig. 1) displays the Boundary, the Core and the quality of approximation of the decision maker. The lower approximation of the class Cl_2 is the difference between the Boundary and all knowledge classified in Cl_2. More details on these steps are available in [13]. Figure 1 shows the results of executing the DRSA method on the data related to the Decision Maker 3 (DM3). Results are as follows:

- DM3's Boundary = B = $\{K_3, K_{10}, K_{13}, K_{14}, K_{15}, K_{20}, K_{23}, K_{24}\}$; $| B | = 8$.
- Knowledge that is classified by DM3 in Cl_2 = K = $\{K_3, K_4, K_5, K_6, K_7,$
  $K_8, K_{10}, K_{12}, K_{13}, K_{15}, K_{16}, K_{18}, K_{19}, K_{20}, K_{21}, K_{22}, K_{24}, K_{26}, K_{27}, K_{29},$
  $K_{30}, K_{31}, K_{32}, K_{33}, K_{34}\}$; $| K | = 25$.
- Lower approximation = LA = K - B = $\{K_4, K_5, K_6, K_7, K_8, K_{12}, K_{16}, K_{18},$
  $K_{19}, K_{21}, K_{22}, K_{26}, K_{27}, K_{29}, K_{30}, K_{31}, K_{32}, K_{33}, K_{34}\}$; $| LA | = 19$.
- Approximation quality of DM3 = $\frac{|LA|}{|K|} = 0.76$
- DM3's Core= $\{g_1, g_2, g_3, g_4, g_6, g_7\}$: DM3 classifies knowledge as "Crucial" because it is easily accessible (g_1), specific (g_2), easily codifiable (g_3), up-to-date (g_4), relevant (g_6) and accurate (g_7), without giving importance to whether it is complete or not, so (g_5) cannot belong to his core.

3.2   Theoretical Method of Explicit and Tacit Knowledge Sharing

The knowledge sharing process that we define is based on a recommendation system (RS) and distinguishes between explicit and tacit knowledge. The RS plays the role of an intermediary between the knowledge transmitter and the knowledge receiver. It takes as inputs the *current decision maker (CDM) query* and the *decision tables of all the system decision makers (DMs)*. At the first use of the RS, each decision maker (DM) must register: he has to enter his personal information and -then- to complete the "column D" about all knowledge classifications. Upon the second use, the DM can use the RS only by submitting his query. This method is based on two steps: applying the collaborative filtering based on DRSA to find a *neighborhood* for the CDM and then using the knowledge based filtering to consider the CDM needs.

Collaborative Filtering Technique Based on DRSA: The collaborative filtering objective is to define *a collection of system DMs having the same taste as the CDM in the past*, called neighborhood. This technique takes as input the set of all decision tables to calculate a *similarity measure* that we define, in our method, using the parameters of *Lower approximation* and *Core* provided by the DRSA method. In fact, two DMs are similar if they classified the same knowledge with certainty as crucial for the same reasons: some knowledge belongs to their Lower approximation (LA) and sometimes they shared the same Core criteria. Based on this idea, our method is based on two selections:

- At the first selection, for each DM we will compute the set of intersection between his LA and that of the CDM. Then, DMs will be ordered in a decreasing way according to the size of the intersection set found.

List 1: *CDM's neighborhood based LA* = $\{DM_1...DM_n;$ such as
$\forall i \in \{1..n\} \mid LA(DM_i) \cap LA(CDM) \mid \geq \mid LA(DM_{i+1}) \cap LA(CDM) \mid\}$
where n is the number of DMs who have at least a knowledge that belongs both to their LA and to that of the CDM.

- The second selection is applied to customize the results of the first list. In fact, if two or more DMs of List 1 have the same size of the set of intersection between their LA and that of the CDM, they will be ordered according to the intersection of their Core and that of the CDM:

List 2: ***CDM's neighborhood based LA & Core*** $= \{DM_1...DM_n;$ such as $\forall i \in \{1..n\}\langle| LA(DM_i) \cap LA(CDM) |\geq| LA(DM_{i+1}) \cap LA(CDM) |$ $\rangle \bigvee \langle| LA(DM_i) \cap LA(CDM) |=| LA(DM_{i+1}) \cap LA(CDM) | \bigwedge |$ $Core(DM_i) \cap Core(CDM) |\geq| Core(DM_{i+1}) \cap Core(CDM) |\rangle\}$

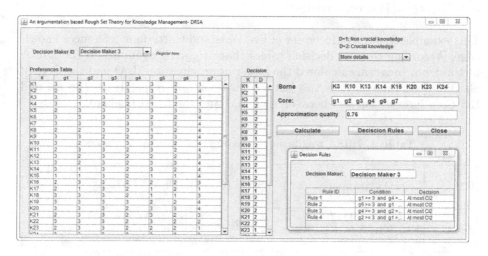

Fig. 1. Decision Table provided by a unique user

Knowledge-Based Filtering Technique: Once the final selective neighborhood (List 2) is determined, the RS gathers all the knowledge that is already appreciated by this neighborhood but not yet seen by the CDM. However, the set of obtained Knowledge may not entirely match the CDM needs. To do so, we apply the knowledge-based filtering to compare the CDM's query with the resulting knowledge metadata in order to recommend only those that satisfy the query. To analyze DMs' queries we have been based on the medical ontology proposed in [7].

Thus, this new recommended knowledge set can construct and enrich the knowledge background of the current user and help him make a right and a revised decision that should be -then- classified by the CDM as crucial or not.

As we already mentioned, our model treats both the explicit and the tacit knowledge. The recommendations must, thus, depend on the knowledge's nature:

- *If the recommended knowledge is explicit:* the system provides the list of obtained knowledge. Then, the user must interpret each of them and transform it into a new explicit knowledge (combination) or into a tacit knowledge (internalization).

– *If the recommended knowledge is tacit:* this knowledge is usually difficult to be articulated or shared. It is generally transferred through face-to-face interactions between persons who hold it. In this case, the recommendation system recommends to the current user the profiles of the stakeholders holding the desired knowledge. It proposes thus- a list of possible meetings according to the stakeholders' availability. If, following a meeting, the tacit knowledge remains difficult to be articulated, it is still held in the DMs' minds (Socialization). Otherwise, it will be transformed into an explicit one (Externalization).

4   Illustrative example

This example treats a reduced set of five DMs and thirty-four references knowledge. According to their decision tables that are given as inputs to the DRSA method, our program calculated the Lower approximation (LA) and the Core of all DMs (see Table 1). The two last columns contain -respectively- the *LA* and the *Core* intersection sets between each DM and the CDM (Celine).

Table 1. DRSA results for the recommendation system users

DM	LowerApproximation (LA)	Core (Co)	DM3'LA ∩ DM'LA	DM3'Co ∩ DM'Co
Jean	$K_1, K_4, K_6, K_7, K_8, K_{11},$ $K_{24}, K_{26}, K_{28}, K_{29}, K_{30},$ K_{31}, K_{32}	$g_1, g_2, g_3,$ g_4, g_6, g_7	$K_4, K_6, K_7, K_8, K_{24},$ $K_{26}, K_{29}, K_{30}, K_{31},$ K_{32}	$g_1, g_2,$ $g_3, g_4,$ g_6, g_7
Mark	$K_2, K_3, K_4, K_5, K_7, K_8, K_9,$ $K_{10}, K_{11}, K_{12}, K_{14}, K_{16},$ $K_{20}, K_{23}, K_{31}, K_{32}, K_{33}$	$g_1, g_2, g_4,$ g_5, g_7	$K_3, K_4, K_5, K_7, K_8,$ $K_{10}, K_{12}, K_{16}, K_{20},$ K_{31}, K_{32}, K_{33}	$g_1, g_2,$ g_4, g_7
Celine (DM3)	$K_3, K_4, K_5, K_6, K_7, K_8,$ $K_{10}, K_{12}, K_{13}, K_{15}, K_{16},$ $K_{18}, K_{19}, K_{20}, K_{21}, K_{22},$ $K_{24}, K_{26}, K_{27}, K_{29}, K_{30},$ $K_{31}, K_{32}, K_{33}, K_{34}$	$g_1, g_2, g_3,$ g_4, g_6, g_7	$K_3, K_4, K_5, K_6, K_7,$ $K_8, K_{10}, K_{12}, K_{13},$ $K_{15}, K_{16}, K_{18}, K_{19},$ $K_{20}, K_{21}, K_{22}, K_{24},$ $K_{26}, K_{27}, K_{29}, K_{30},$ $K_{31}, K_{32}, K_{33}, K_{34}$	$g_1, g_2,$ $g_3, g_4,$ g_6, g_7
Abdel	$K_3, K_4, K_6, K_8, K_{10}, K_{11},$ $K_{15}, K_{16}, K_{17}, K_{19}, K_{22},$ $K_{24}, K_{26}, K_{27}, K_{30}, K_{33}$	$g_2, g_3, g_4,$ g_5, g_6	$K_3, K_4, K_8, K_{10}, K_{15},$ $K_{16}, K_{19}, K_{22}, K_{24},$ $K_{26}, K_{27}, K_{30}, K_{33}$	$g_2, g_3,$ g_4, g_6
Paul	$K_1, K_2, K_5, K_6, K_8, K_9,$ $K_{11}, K_{12}, K_{13}, K_{15}, K_{21}, K_{24},$ $K_{27}, K_{28}, K_{30}, K_{31}, K_{34}$	$g_1, g_2, g_4,$ g_6, g_7	$K_5, K_6, K_8, K_{12}, K_{13},$ $K_{15}, K_{21}, K_{24}, K_{27},$ K_{30}, K_{31}, K_{34}	$g_1, g_2,$ g_4, g_6, g_7

Table 2 details the first table. Its last column contains the new knowledge that has already been appreciated by the DMs. So, our RS runs as follow:

– Applying the Collaborative filtering based Lower Approximation: we get an ordered list of decision-makers according to the size of the intersection set of their lower approximations and that of the current decision-maker. So:

The first selection = List 1= $\{Abdel, Mark, Paul, Jean\}$;

- Applying the Collaborative filtering based Core: The first ordered list (List 1) must be ordered according to the size of the intersection set of the decision makers' Core and that of the current decision-maker. So:

The second selection= List 2= $\{Abdel, Paul, Mark, Jean\}$;

- Generating the knowledge list that have been appreciated by the decision-makers in List 2 respecting their order:

List 3 = $\{ K_{43}, K_{46}, K_{52}, K_{46}, K_{47}, K_{51}, K_{43}, K_{48}, K_{50}, K_{46} \}$;

- Removing redundancy in List 3:

List 4 = $\{ K_{43}, K_{46}, K_{52}, K_{47}, K_{51}, K_{48}, K_{50} \}$;

- Using Knowledge-based Filtering: This step is based on the matching between the knowledge metadata and the current DM query. If we suppose that the metadata available on knowledge are ⟨Knowledge holder, Knowledge domain, Knowledge user⟩. So, descriptions that we have on the List 4's knowledge are:
  • K_{43} = ⟨Dr Elene, Pediatrics Neurology, Child⟩
  • K_{46} = ⟨Pr Layla, Physical therapy, Both⟩
  • K_{52} = ⟨Dr Marylene, Speech therapy, Both⟩
  • K_{47} = ⟨Dr Agnes, Neurology, Adult⟩
  • K_{51} = ⟨Pr Florence, Pediatrics Neurology, Child⟩
  • K_{48} = ⟨Pr Pierre, Speech therapy, Adult⟩
  • K_{50} = ⟨Dr Mathieu, Pediatrics Neurology, Child⟩

Table 2. A summary for decision-makers results compared to those of (DM3)

Decision maker (DM)	$\mid DM3'LA \cap DM'LA \mid$	$\mid DM3'Co \cap DM'Co \mid$	Knowledge appreciated by DM
Jean	10	6	K_{46}
Mark	12	4	K_{43}, K_{48}, K_{50}
Abdel	13	4	K_{43}, K_{46}, K_{52}
Paul	12	5	K_{46}, K_{47}, K_{51}

We suppose, now, that the query submitted by Celine (DM3) is as follow: **How to examine the cranial nerves of a child?**. Thus, if we consider the medical ontology proposed by [7], we find that the "cranial nerves exam" is a process in the pediatric Neurology domain that concerns children. Therefore, our system should recommend to Celine only the ordered list of knowledge whose "domain" is that of Pediatrics Neurology and whose "user" is the child.

$$\boxed{\text{Final recommended List} = \{K_{43}, K_{51}, K_{50}\}}$$

Finally, the current user (Celine) has to evaluate the three recommended knowledge. She has just to say if any one was "Crucial" or "not crucial".

5   Conclusion

In this paper, we have proposed a theoretical method of organizational knowledge sharing based on a recommendation system that relies on a multicriteria decision aid method to improve the explicit and tacit knowledge sharing processes. We relied on the collaborative filtering based-DRSA to identify the current decision maker's neighborhood, and the knowledge-based filtering to match the current decision maker's query with the knowledge profile. In order to implement the DRSA method, we proposed a set of evaluation criteria. Our goal is to improve the knowledge sharing among the medical staff to help them consolidate their decisions in complex clinical circumstances. Our future work will be, thus, to validate our method on a medical field that is of the APMDS. We will, first, involve the experts of this association in order to validate the evaluation criteria. Then, we will exploit the mobile learning methods and the Web 2.0 technology such as the social networks or the forums to organize meetings between the system users and to enhance the tacit knowledge transfer. Finally, we will have to implement our automated recommendation system for knowledge sharing.

References

1. Belton, V., Pictet, J.: A framework for group decision using mcda model: sharing aggregation or comparing individual information. Revue des Systemes de Decision **6**, 283–303 (1997)
2. Boisot, M.: Information Space: A Framework for Learning in Organizations, Institutions and Culture. Routledge, Thomson Learning Emea, London (1995)
3. Burke, R.: Hybrid recommender systems: survey and experiments. User Model User-Adap. Inter. **12**(4), 331–370 (2002)
4. Burke, R., Hammond, K., Cooper, E.: Knowledge based navigation of complex information spaces. In: Proceedings of the 13th National Conference on Artificial Intelligence (AAAI 1996), Menlo Park, pp. 462–468 (1996)
5. Davenport, T.H., Prusak, L.: Working Knowledge: How Organizations Manage What They Know. Harvard Business School Press, Boston (1998)
6. Dubois, D., Prade, H.: Possibility Theory: An Approach To Computerized Processing Of Uncertainty. Plenum Press, New York (1988)
7. Ghrab, S., Saad, I., Kassel, G., Gargouri, F.: COOK: A Core ontology of knowhow and knowing-that to measure organization know-how and knowing-that. In: KMIKS (2015)
8. Goldberg, D., Nichols, D., Oki, B.M., Terry, D.: Using collaborative filtering to weave an information tapestry. ACM Commun. **35**(12), 61–70 (1992)
9. Greco, S., Matarazzo, S., Slowinski, S.: Rough sets theory for multicriteria decision analysis. Eur. J. Oper. Res. **129**, 1–47 (2001)
10. Pawlak, Z.: Rough sets. Int. J. Comput. Sci. **11**, 341–356 (1992)
11. Nonaka, I.: Creating organizational order out of chaos: self- renewal in Japanese firms. Calif. Manag. Rev. **15**(3), 57–73 (1988)
12. Quinlan, J.R.: C4.5: Programs for Machine Learning. Morgan Kaufmann, San Mateo (1993)
13. Chakhar, S., Saad, I.: A decision support for identifying crucial knowledge requiring capitalizing operation. Eur. J. Oper. Res. **195**(3), 889–904 (2009). doi:10.1016/j.ejor.2007.11.021

14. Wang, R.Y., Strong, D.M.: Beyond accuracy: what data quality means to data consumers. J. Manag. Inf. Syst. **12**(4), 5–34 (1996)
15. Wang, R.Y., Strong, D.M.: Knowing-why about data processes and data quality. J. Manag. Inf. Syst. **20**(3), 13–39 (2003)

A Collaborative Spatial Decision Support System for the Capacitated Vehicle Routing Problem on a Tabletop Display

Nikolaos Ploskas[1]($\boxtimes$), Ioannis Athanasiadis[2], Jason Papathanasiou[1], and Nikolaos Samaras[1]

[1] University of Macedonia, 156 Egnatia Str., 54006 Thessaloniki, Greece
{ploskas,jasonp,samaras}@uom.gr
[2] Hellenic Open University, 8 Ptolemaion Str., 50100 Kozani, Greece
g-athan@hotmail.com

Abstract. The Vehicle Routing Problem (VRP) is a well-known combinatorial optimization problem. The Capacitated Vehicle Routing Problem (CVRP) is a widely studied variant of the VRP. Although many Decision Support Systems (DSS) have been implemented to support decision makers solve real life problems of the VRP and its variants, these systems do not allow multiple decision makers to collaborate with each other and explore different scenarios on a specific problem. Recent advances in hardware and software have enabled a new generation of tabletop displays that can sense multiple inputs from different users at the same time. In this paper, we present a collaborative spatial DSS for the CVRP on a tabletop display that allows two decision makers to collaborate with each other in order to find the best possible solution. The locations of the customers to serve are added using interactive Google Maps. The DSS extracts the geographical information of the selected locations, finds the distances between them and solves the problem. The proposed DSS has been implemented using Java, TUIO protocol, jsprit and Google Maps.

Keywords: Decision support systems · Capacitated vehicle routing problem · Tabletop · Tangible user interface · Geographical information systems

1 Introduction

The Vehicle Routing Problem (VRP) is a well-studied combinatorial optimization problem in the field of transportation logistics [17,27]. VRP has been initially introduced by Dantzig and Ramser [8]. Many variants of the VRP have been proposed since then. The Capacitated Vehicle Routing Problem (CVRP) is a well-known variant of the VRP and is an NP-hard problem. The objective is to determine a viable route schedule, which minimizes the distance or the total cost, for a number of vehicles starting from a central depot to a number

© Springer International Publishing Switzerland 2015
I. Linden et al. (Eds.): EWG-DSS 2014, LNBIP 221, pp. 26–36, 2015.
DOI: 10.1007/978-3-319-21536-5_3

of customers, and then return to the depot. Each customer must be served once by one vehicle and the total demand of any route must not exceed the capacity of the vehicle.

VRP was addressed by many authors and several algorithms and methods were proposed to solve its different variants. The algorithms and methods that have been proposed fall into two categories: (i) exact algorithms, and (ii) approximate algorithms. In the first category, most research focused on developing branch-and-cut methods [4,18]. Another exact algorithm is the branch and-cut-and-price algorithm proposed by Fukasawa et al. [10] (for a detailed survey of exact algorithms for the CVRP, see [20,28]). In the second category, many heuristics and metaheuristics have been proposed (for a detailed survey of approximate algorithms for the CVRP, see [6,16]).

Many software packages and DSS exist for the solution of the VRP and its variants exclusively. Only few of them integrate real-life geographical information of the customers' locations using interactive maps [2,12,13,22,23,26]. Anderson et al. [1] used a tabletop display in the solution of the Capacitated Vehicle Routing Problem with Time Windows (CVRPTW). To the best of our knowledge, this is the first paper that proposes a collaborative spatial DSS for the CVRP on a tabletop display. The innovation of this paper is that we implement a collaborative spatial DSS for the CVRP on a tabletop display that can assist decision-makers to collaborate with each other and explore different scenarios on a specific problem.

The structure of the paper is as follows. Section 2 presents some key features about the tangible user interfaces, a brief review of the use of tangible user interfaces on decision-making process and the principles of the constructed tabletop. Section 3 briefly presents the mathematical form of the problem, while in Sect. 4 the analysis and implementations steps of the collaborative spatial DSS are presented. Finally, the conclusions of this paper are outlined in Sect. 5.

2   Tangible User Interfaces

A tabletop is a computing device that offers a large, horizontal digital display and enables one or more users to input commands to the device by interacting directly with the display surface [24]. A tabletop offers a useful shared space for diverse collaborative tasks. The key idea of the tabletop displays is the replacement of the traditional input devices (e.g. mouse, keyboard) with more natural and interactive devices. A tabletop can be handled either by finger and hand gestures or by controller objects. In this paper, we use both approaches; customers' locations are specified using controller objects and more specifically fiducials, and the other parameters are given through finger and hand gestures. Fiducials are markers used to recognize object. Two types of fiducials exist: (i) active, (ii) and passive. Passive fiducials are images that can be recognized through a camera. An example of a passive fiducial is shown in Fig. 1.

According to Müller–Tomfelde [19], there will be an increasing adoption of tabletop systems in the next decade. This becomes more evident if we focus

Fig. 1. Example of passive fiducial

on the tabletop's Hype Cycle [19], where we may notice the clear shift to the productivity phase of the technology.

Tabletop displays have been widely used in decision-making process. Kientz et al. [15] proposed a DSS to support collaborative decision-making for home-based therapy teams. Scotta et al. [25] presented a multi-user tangible interface system that aims at introducing an instrument to improve the response phase of the decision-making process. Hofstra et al. [11] used multi-user tangible interfaces for decision-making in disaster management. Scott et al. [24] have used table-top interfaces to support collaborative decision-making in maritime operations. Engelbrecht et al. [9] used digital tabletops for situational awareness in emergency situations. In our previous work [21], we used the same collaborative tabletop interface to support decision-making for the solution of the multiple capacitated facility location problem. The proposed paper uses the same tabletop interface with our previous work [21], but solves another problem (VRP) and uses different collaborative strategies.

Most of the aforementioned papers have used commercial tabletop interfaces. The tabletop used in this paper has been designed and constructed from scratch. We designed our own tabletop instead of using a commercial tabletop interface, because commercial tabletop interfaces allow multiple gestures and the use of a pen to draw upon them, but do not support the use of several fiducials for the recognition of different objects in the tabletop interface. Figure 2 shows the interior and the exterior of the designed tabletop.

The most significant constraints and parameters of the construction were:

- The need to support multi–touch and object recognition.
- Its physical characteristics were devised with the aim of promoting collocated collaboration of two decision makers.
- The absence of need for user awareness and shared working space.

The whole system consists of two separate subsystems. The first one refers to the image projection system and the second to the input capturing system (multi–touch and object recognition). The input capturing system uses the infrared light as a means of input identification in order to avoid interference with the image projection. The key design features of this tabletop are (for a more detailed description, see [3]):

- Diffused Surface Illumination (DSI) was used to construct the tabletop, because it recognizes objects and fiducials and there are no illumination hotspots due to the even illumination throughout the surface.
- 85 cm height.
- 42 inches display.
- A sort throw Benq MS612ST projector was used with a throw ratio of 0.90–1.08.
- An endlighten acrylic with infrared leds on each side of it.
- Two modified infrared cameras in a row, supporting 120 fps for 320×240 resolution and 60 fps for 640×480 resolution each, with a lens focusing distance of 2.8 mm.

(a) Inside View of the Tabletop   (b) Overview of the Tabletop

Fig. 2. The constructed tabletop

3   Problem Specification

The CVRP can be described as follows: Products are to be delivered to a number of customers by a fleet of identical vehicles starting from a central depot. The objective is to determine a viable route schedule, which minimizes the distance or the total cost with the following constraints:

- Each vehicle starts and ends its route at the central depot.
- Each customer should be served once by one vehicle.
- The total demand of each route must not exceed the capacity of each vehicle.
- The total length of each route must not exceed a fixed length.

Let us assume that the central depot is node 0 and V vehicles should serve N customers. Let us denote with d_i the demand of customer i and c_v the capacity of vehicle v. The maximum allowed total length of the route served by vehicle v is denoted with L_v and the cost travelling from customer i to customer j by vehicle v is C_{ij}^v. The mathematical form of this problem based on the formulation given by Bodin et al. [5] can be formulated as follows:

$$min \sum_{v=1}^{V} \sum_{i=0}^{N} \sum_{j=0}^{N} C_{ij}^v X_{ij}^v \tag{1}$$

subject to

$$X_{ij}^v = \begin{cases} 1, \text{ if vehicle v travels from customer i to j} \\ 0, \text{ otherwise} \end{cases} \tag{2}$$

$$\sum_{v=1}^{V} \sum_{i=0}^{N} X_{ij}^v = 1, j = 1, 2, ..., N \tag{3}$$

$$\sum_{v=1}^{V} \sum_{j=0}^{N} X_{ij}^v = 1, i = 1, 2, ..., N \tag{4}$$

$$\sum_{i=0}^{N} X_{it}^v - \sum_{j=0}^{N} X_{tj}^v = 0, v = 1, 2, ..., V \text{ and } t = 1, 2, ..., N \tag{5}$$

$$\sum_{i=0}^{N} \sum_{j=0}^{N} d_{ij}^v X_{ij}^v \le L_v, v = 1, 2, ..., V \tag{6}$$

$$\sum_{j=0}^{N} c_j \left(\sum_{i=0}^{N} X_{ij}^v \right) \le c_v, v = 1, 2, ..., V \tag{7}$$

$$\sum_{i=1}^{N} X_{0j}^v \le 1, v = 1, 2, ..., V \tag{8}$$

$$\sum_{j=1}^{N} X_{i0}^v \le 1, v = 1, 2, ..., V \tag{9}$$

Objective function (1) refers to the minimization of the total cost. Constraint (2) ensures that the variable X_{ij}^v takes the integer 0 or 1. Constraints (3) and (4) ensure that each customer is served once. Constraint (5) ensures the route continuity, while Constraint (6) refers to the maximum allowed fixed length of each route. Constraint (7) ensures that the total demand of each route will not exceed the capacity of each vehicle, while Constraints (8) and (9) ensure that each vehicle is used only once.

4   Design, Implementation and Presentation of the DSS

Figure 3 presents the decision making process that the decision makers can perform using the DSS. Initially, the decision makers select the location of the central depot via an interactive Google Map using fiducials on the tabletop (Fig. 4a). Then, the decision makers select the location of the customers (Fig. 4b) and for each customer input the demand quantity and the service time (Fig. 5). After

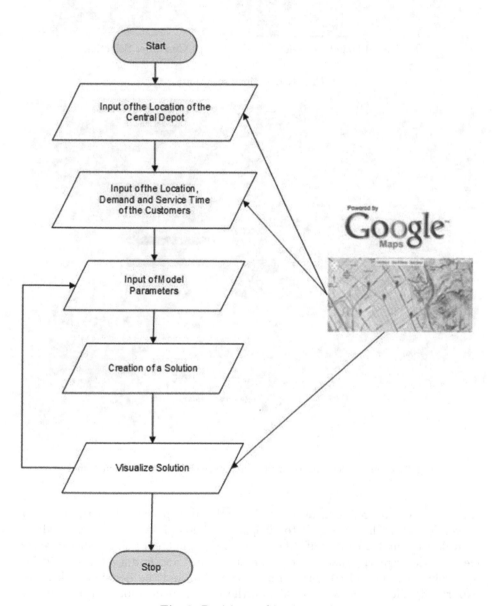

Fig. 3. Decision making process

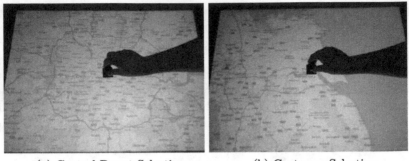

(a) Central Depot Selection   (b) Customer Selection

Fig. 4. Locations selection

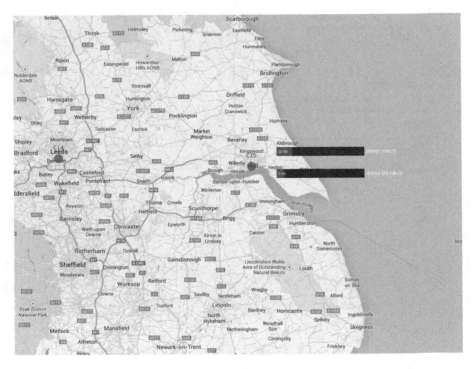

Fig. 5. Input of demand quantity and service time for each customer

this step the final representation of the problem is presented to the decision makers (Fig. 6). Then, the tabletop display is divided into two segments, where each decision maker can input different model parameters (i.e. number of vehicles, vehicles' capacity, fixed cost, and cost per km) and find a solution (Fig. 7). The solution is visualized through a Google Map and the decision maker can export a detailed report as a pdf file. Furthermore, one decision maker can press

Fig. 6. Final representation of the problem

the share button in order to copy his/her model parameters and solution to the other decision maker's display.

Let us give an insight to the collaboration procedure that we have adopted in this implementation. Two decision makers can work on the same problem and find alternatives for its solution. At any time, the decision makers can compare their solutions and keep the best one by pressing the share button (Fig. 7). Then, decision makers can work to improve the found solution by adjusting the problem's parameters (e.g. editing the number of vehicles or the fixed cost) and explore new alternatives. When a final solution is found for the problem, then the decision makers can press the report button to export a detailed report.

The spatial DSS has been implemented using Java, TUIO, jsprit and Google Maps. More specifically, the open source TUIO protocol [14] has been utilized in order to recognize a set of objects with fiducials and draw gestures onto the table surface with the finger tips. TUIO protocol is encoded using Open Sound Control format and the transport method is made through UDP packets to the default TUIO port number 3333. Furthermore, jsprit [13], a java based, open source toolkit for solving rich traveling salesman (TSP) and VRP variants, has been utilized in order to find a solution for the given problems.

Community Core Vision (CCV), previously known as tbeta, is an open source software that takes as input a video stream and outputs several tracking data, such as coordinates of the objects or events like finger down [7]. CCV was selected compared to reacTIVision and Touchlib, because CCV has more filter options. The recognition of the camera from CCV requires the installation of the device driver named CL-EYE Platform Driver. Moreover, open source Unfolding library [29] for Java was used to create interactive Google Maps and geovisualizations.

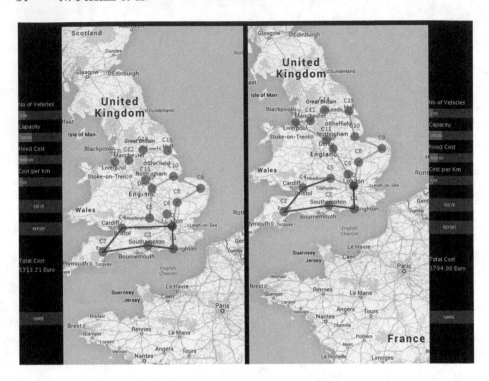

Fig. 7. Visualization of the solutions

The library supports various functions to get automatically the distance in km between two points in the earth.

5   Conclusions

The VRP is a well-known combinatorial optimization problem with many practical applications. Collaborative DSS using tabletop displays have not yet been used for this problem. In this paper, we present a collaborative spatial DSS for the CVRP on a tabletop display that allows two decision makers to collaborate with each other in order to find the best possible solution. The locations of the customers to serve are added using interactive Google Maps. The DSS extracts the geographical information of the selected locations, find the distances between them and solves the problem according to the specified model parameters of each decision maker. The solution of the problem is presented both on an interactive Google Map and on a pdf file. Decision makers can compare their solutions, collaborate to improve one solution by adjusting problem's parameters and find the best possible one.

In future work, we plan to include other VRP variants in order to enhance the DSS with other options. Furthermore, we plan to make a study in order to examine the collaboration aspects of the proposed DSS and enhanced them if possible.

References

1. Anderson, D., Anderson, E., Lesh, N., Marks, J., Mirtich, B., Ratajczak, D., Ryall, K.: Human-guided simple search. In: Seventeenth National Conference on Artificial Intelligence Conference Proceedings (AAAI-00), pp. 209–216 (2000)
2. ArcGIS. http://www.esri.com/software/arcgis. Accessed 4 October 2014
3. Athanasiadis, I.: Analysis, Design and Implementation of a Hybrid System for Teaching Basic Programming Structures using Traditional and Tangible User Interfaces to Pre Teenagers. MSc Thesis, School of Science and Technology, Hellenic Open University (2014)
4. Blasum, U., Hochstttler, W.: Application of the branch and cut method to the vehicle routing problem. Technical report zpr2000-386, Zentrum fur Angewandte Informatik Koln (2000)
5. Bodin, L., Golden, B.L., Assad, A., Ball, M.O.: The state of the art in the routing and scheduling of vehicles and crews. Comput. Oper. Res. **10**, 69–221 (1983)
6. Cordeau, J.F., Gendreau, M., Hertz, A., Laporte, G., Sormany, J.S.: New heuristics for the vehicle routing problem. In: Langevin, A., Riopel, D. (eds.) Logistics Systems: Design And Optimization, pp. 279–297. Springer, New York (2005)
7. Community Core Vision. http://nuicode.com/projects/tbeta. Accessed 4 October 2014
8. Dantzig, G.B., Ramser, R.H.: The truck dispatching problem. Manage. Sci. **6**, 80–91 (1959)
9. Engelbrecht, A., Borges, M., Vivacqua, A.S.: Digital tabletops for situational awareness in emergency situations. In: 15th International Conference Proceedings on Computer Supported Cooperative Work in Design (CSCWD), pp. 669–676 (2011)
10. Fukasawa, R., Longo, H., Lysgaard, J., de Arago, M.P., Reis, M., Uchoa, E., Werneck, R.F.: Robust branch-and-cut-and-price for the capacitated vehicle routing problem. Math. Program. **106**(3), 491–511 (2006)
11. Hofstra, H., Scholten, H., Zlatanova, S., Scotta, A.: Multi-user tangible interfaces for effective decision-making in disaster management. In: Nayak, S., Zlatanova, S. (eds.) Remote Sensing And Gis Technologies For Monitoring And Prediction Of Disasters, pp. 243–266. Springer, Berlin (2008)
12. Ioannou, G., Kritikos, M.N., Prastacos, G.P.: Map-Route: a GIS-based decision support system for intra-city vehicle routing with time windows. J. Oper. Res. Soc. **53**, 842–854 (2002)
13. jsprit. https://github.com/jsprit/jsprit. Accessed 4 October 2014
14. Kaltenbrunner, M., Bovermann, T., Bencina, R., Costanza, E.: TUIO - a protocol for table-top tangible user interfaces. In: 6th International Workshop on Gesture in Human-Computer Interaction and Simulation Proceedings (2005)
15. Kientz, J.A., Hayes, G.R., Abowd, G.D., Grinter, R.E.: From the war room to the living room: decision support for home-based therapy teams. In: 20th Anniversary Conference on Computer Supported Cooperative Work Proceedings, pp. 209–218 (2006)
16. Laporte, G., Semet, F.: Classical heuristics for the capacitated VRP. In: Toth, P., Vigo, D. (eds.) The Vehicle Routing Problem. SIAM Monographs on Discrete Mathematics and Applications, vol. 9(5), pp. 109–128. Society for Industrial and Applied Mathematics, Philadelphia (2002)
17. Laporte, G.: Fifty years of vehicle routing. Transp. Sci. **43**(4), 408–416 (2009)

18. Lysgaard, J., Letchford, A.N., Eglese, R.W.: A new branch-and-cut algorithm for the capacitated vehicle routing problem. Math. Program. **100**(2), 423–445 (2004)
19. Müller-Tomfelde, C., Fjeld, M.: Tabletops: interactive horizontal displays for ubiquitous computing. Computer **2**, 78–81 (2012)
20. Naddef, D., Rinaldi, G.: Branch-and-Cut algorithms for the capacitated VRP. In: Toth, P., Vigo, D. (eds.) The Vehicle Routing Problem. SIAM Monographs on Discrete Mathematics and Applications, vol. 9, pp. 53–84. Society for Industrial and Applied Mathematics, Philadelphia (2002)
21. Ploskas, N., Athanasiadis, I., Papathanasiou, J., Samaras, N.: An Interactive Spatial Decision Support System Enabling Co-Located Collaboration using Tangible User Interfaces for the Multiple Capacitated Facility Location Problem. International Journal of Decision Support System Technology, submitted for publication (2015)
22. Ruiz, R., Maroto, C., Alcaraz, J.: A decision support system for a real vehicle routing problem. Eur. J. Oper. Res. **153**(3), 593–606 (2004)
23. Santos, L., Coutinho-Rodrigues, J., Antunes, C.H.: A web spatial decision support system for vehicle routing using Google Maps. Decis. Support Syst. **51**(1), 1–9 (2011)
24. Scott, S.D., Allavena, A., Cerar, K., Franck, G., Hazen, M., Shuter, T., Colliver, C.: Investigating tabletop interfaces to support collaborative decision-making in maritime operations. In: International Command and Control Research and Technology Symposium Proceedings (ICCRTS 2010), pp. 22–24 (2010)
25. Scotta, A., Pleizier, I.D., Scholten, H.J.: Tangible user interfaces in order to improve collaborative interactions and decision making. In: 25th Urban Data Management Symposium Proceedings, pp. 15–17 (2006)
26. Tarantilis, C.D., Kiranoudis, C.T.: Using a spatial decision support system for solving the vehicle routing problem. Inf. Manage. **39**(5), 359–375 (2002)
27. Toth, P., Vigo, D.: The Vehicle Routing Problem. Siam, Philadelphia (2001)
28. Toth, P., Vigo, D.: Branch-and-bound algorithms for the capacitated VRP. In: Toth, P., Vigo, D. (eds.) The Vehicle Routing Problem. SIAM Monographs on Discrete Mathematics and Applications, pp. 29–51. Society for Industrial and Applied Mathematics, Philadelphia (2002)
29. Unfolding. http://unfoldingmaps.org/. Accessed 4 October 2014

Trust and Understanding in Face-to-Face and Online Negotiations

Yvonne van der Toorn[✉], Per van der Wijst, and Debby Damen

Department of Communication and Information Sciences, Tilburg University,
P.O. Box 90153, 5000 LE Tilburg, The Netherlands
yvonnevandertoorn@gmail.com

Abstract. This study investigates the effects of social presence and synchronicity on the creation of mutual trust and understanding between conflicting parties in negotiations. An experimental study was conducted in which participants negotiated either face-to-face, through synchronous chat or through asynchronous e-mail. The results show that the high social presence in FtF communication seems to enhance the feelings of trust and understanding the negotiator has in the other party compared to the online negotiations, but not the amount of understanding and trust the other party has in him/her. Synchronicity does not seem to have an influence on the negotiation processes since both the synchronous chat and the asynchronous e-mail condition have equal scores on mutual trust and understanding.

Keywords: Negotiation · Trust · Understanding · Synchronicity · CMC · Chat · E-mail · Face-to-face

1 Introduction

The words 'trust' and 'understanding' are often used in the context of relationships and seem to be essential for healthy relations. It is therefore not surprising that studies have indicated that understanding is an essential factor for a mutually acceptable resolution in *negotiations* [1, 2]. Rather than fundamental differences of interest, the sources of a conflict are mostly a lack of misunderstanding or failures to understand [2]. In most negotiations, solving the differences of view is a great challenge, but understanding them is an important first step on the way to a solution. To understand the nature of a dispute, there are different versions of meaning to be explored, rather than sets of facts to be discovered [3]. In addition to mutual understanding, trust between conflicting parties has proven to be a key factor for the success of a negotiation [4]. Trust is generally demonstrated by a willingness of parties to place themselves in some position of risk in a negotiation, such as by being open with information sharing [4]. Parties who trust each other approach each other with cooperative dispositions which leads to more cooperative behavior within the negotiation. In turn, greater expectations of trust lead to greater information sharing with the other party and it is especially this information sharing that facilitates mutual understanding among parties. Therefore, trust is generally known to be a prerequisite to information sharing and cooperative behavior [5–7], which ultimately increases the chances on a mutually beneficial outcome. Without

© Springer International Publishing Switzerland 2015
I. Linden et al. (Eds.): EWG-DSS 2014, LNBIP 221, pp. 37–50, 2015.
DOI: 10.1007/978-3-319-21536-5_4

trust, individuals are less likely to take the risks implied by cooperative behavior and are more inclined towards competitive behavior [8].

The upcoming of the Internet and digital communication have increased the popularity of online communication for all kind of purposes, including negotiations. Different studies have shown that online communication has a serious impact on the factors of mutual understanding and trust [8–10]. According to the Social Presence Theory [11], FtF communication is considered to have the most social presence whereas text-based communication has the least. In situations where the environment does not provide opportunities for social cues relevant for normal behavior (situation with low social presence), fewer constraints on counter-normative behavior are observed [12]. Computer-mediated communication (CMC), which is mostly text-based and therefore has a low social presence, has been associated with counter-normative social behavior [12]. Thus, the relative anonymity and safety of the online environment give easily rise to flaming and other negative and counter-normative forms of communication [13]. The lack of social cues such as facial expressions, gestures, posture, voice tones and eye contact in online communication can also negatively influence the feelings of trust since people heavily rely on these indicators when assessing another's sincerity [14]. When non-verbal information is unavailable, negotiators tend to engage in bluffs, exaggerations and lies [15], which in turn violate feelings of trust for both parties. However, computer-mediated communication has also shown great advantages. Spears and Lea [16] demonstrated that CMC can enhance positive behavior. The individuals are 'uncontaminated' by the physical presence of the other party. This absence of social presence and the characteristic of visual anonymity can encourage negative behavior, but it can also allow for more self-disclosure [16] which could lead to more understanding and trust and might ultimately lead to a more satisfying outcome in negotiations. These opposing effects will be addressed in the present study.

In addition to the influence of social presence on trust and understanding, earlier studies have also shown the importance of distinguishing CMC based on synchronicity. Media Synchronicity can be defined as "the extent to which a communication environment encourages individuals to work together on the same activity, with the same information, at the same time" [17]. Earlier studies have mainly focused on comparing asynchronous CMC to FtF communication. For example, Walther and Burgoon [18] investigated the effects of synchronous FtF communication and asynchronous CMC on relational communication and indicated that the time delays in asynchronous CMC lead to different patterns of relationship development compared to FtF communication. In FtF communication the participants experienced higher levels of psychic, sensory and emotional involvement, increased cognitive load and greater investment in outcomes [18]. This suggests that mutual trust and understanding would be higher in a FtF context. This is supported by studies that [6, 19, 20] investigated the differences between asynchronous (e-mail) and FtF communication in a negotiation setting and that demonstrated the greater challenges for rapport building in e-mail negotiation compared to FtF negotiation. Thompson and Nadler [20] mention several biases that constitute a threat to successful communication in e-negotiations. The temporal synchrony bias seems particularly relevant to understand the assumptions people have when communicating asynchronously. The tendency for e-communicators and also for e-negotiators is to behave as if they are in a synchronous situation, expecting prompt reactions from the addressee. Silences that occur because of the a-synchronous communication mode are generally interpreted as a signal of lack of interest and can yield a negative mindset. In addition, the study of Morris et al. [21] showed that there is less turn-taking behavior in asynchronous negotiations in comparison to FtF negotiations. This is most likely due to the longer messages in negotiations by e-mail. However, turn taking is positively correlated with schmoozing behavior, which in turn leads to trust and rapport [20]. Moreover, the asynchronous nature of the medium and the lack of turn taking is a breading place for misinterpretations. Negotiating asynchronously reduces the opportunity to ask for a clarification during the conversation. Therefore, the communicative contributions of negotiators engaged in asynchronous communication can lead more easily to egocentric and negative assumptions about the other, which ultimately increases the chances that negative emotions like anger start dominating the interaction [21].

These studies have mainly focused on comparing FtF communication to asynchronous CMC communication. To clearly understand the effects of the communication mode on negotiation processes, it is important to not only focus on asynchronous CMC but also on synchronous CMC. Synchronous CMC is closer to FtF communication since it also proceeds in real-time, therefore, one might expect more positive results from synchronous CMC rather than from asynchronous CMC. However, in their study, Pesendorfer and Koeszegi [22] analyzed two e-negotiation simulations in synchronous and asynchronous communication modes. The synchronous negotiation mode led to less friendly and more competitive negotiation behavior while the asynchronous led to more exchange of private and task-oriented information and to a more friendly communication style. In addition, negotiators in asynchronous mode are more satisfied with the process and outcome of the negotiation. This lead Pesendorfer and Koeszegi to conclude that the earlier mentioned counter-normative behavior and other escalating effects that can occur in CMC might be caused by the communication mode rather than by the ability of the medium to transmit social cues. In addition, Walther and Bagoon [18] suggest that the nature of asynchronous communication may also provide the communicator with less stressful conversational demands, allowing increased opportunity and flexibility. You can plan, contemplate and edit one's comments more easily than in synchronous communication, which by definition yields more spontaneous communication and often simultaneous threads of communication. Asynchronous communication may allow users to be more mindful and deliberative in their message construction and they have more time to construct the messages around their ideas and sentiments, for which they completely have to rely on the language that translates those ideas.

The central question in this study is to unravel the effects of social presence and synchronicity on the creation of mutual trust and understanding in negotiations. The set-up of this study aims to fill the gap between the studies that either focus on asynchronous e-mail negotiations compared to synchronous chat, or on FtF negotiations compared to e-negotiations (either synchronous or a-synchronous). We will compare both aspects explicitly in three separate conditions of negotiations: FtF, synchronous chat and a-synchronous e-mail. The earlier mentioned studies have shown that both a rich social presence and a high synchronicity of communication mode are beneficial for mutual trust and understanding during negotiations. The question arises now whether these effects are additive or whether they interact? Since communicating face-to-face has the highest form of social presence and is the most synchronous, we assume that compared to chat negotiation and e-mail negotiation, a FtF negotiation will yield the highest level of mutual trust and understanding:

H1:   Negotiating face-to-face will yield higher levels of mutual trust and understanding than both of the online negotiation conditions

From the two CMC conditions, chat negotiations resemble FtF negotiations most, since both media allow synchronous communication. The synchronicity of the medium allows for the creation of more understanding because the communicators can ask for clarification at any point, immediately when problems occur. However, the synchronicity of the medium also entails the risk of direct impulsive negative communication. In asynchronous e-mail on the other hand, negotiators have the opportunity to be more mindful and think twice about their message construction and they have more time to construct the messages around their ideas and sentiments. Chat negotiators can respond more spontaneously and could therefore be more easily inclined to engage in counter-normative behavior. This counter-normative behavior negatively influences the feelings of trust. Based on this, the following hypotheses are formulated:

H2:   Negotiating synchronously by chat will result in higher mutual understanding than negotiating asynchronously by e-mail

H3:   Negotiating synchronously by chat will result in lower mutual trust than negotiating asynchronously by e-mail

We studied theses hypotheses in a series of simulated negotiation experiments.

2   Methodology

2.1   Participants

Seventy-five people (28 male and 47 female) participated in the study. All participants were communication students from Tilburg University who received a credit point in exchange for their participation. The ages ranged from 18 to 25 with an average of 21.25 (SD = 2.29). The participants were randomly assigned to either the FtF negotiation (N = 19) the chat negotiation (N = 20) or the email negotiation (N = 36). The study consists of a simulation experiment with students as participants, most of them having little negotiation experience.

In both the online chat and the FtF condition, the participants negotiated with confederates to ensure commitment to the negotiation. Four confederates (2 male and 2 female) were instructed to engage actively in the negotiation in order to avoid a simple exchange of objectives and a quick settlement. They were trained to anticipate on the participants' behavior to make sure the level of conflict was similar in each negotiation. During the whole experiment the notion that the confederate was also a participant was upheld. The confederates were randomly assigned to the conditions but the male-female ratio between participant and confederate was counterbalanced. All confederates received financial remuneration for their contribution.

In the e-mail condition, the 36 participants formed 18 dyads who negotiated asynchronously via e-mail. It was decided not to use confederates in this session, because of the logistics of the study. One e-mail negotiation could last for a week. Working with a limited number of confederates who negotiated over several consecutive weeks would be too time-consuming. The option of having confederates running more than one parallel e-negotiation was also considered undesirable because of carry-over effects. For those reasons, we decided to ask different participants for each of the negotiation roles. The dyads consisted of eight all female couples and ten mixed-gender couples. Although most of the participants were native speakers of Dutch, five English-speaking foreign participants participated in the study. They were either coupled to another English speaking foreign participant or to an English speaking native Dutch participant.

2.2 Material

For the experiments a 2.5 page long conflict scenario was developed, based on a similar scenario used by professional negotiation trainers. The original case describes a conflict between two neighbors from a third person's perspective consequently using the last name and both gender abbreviations (Mr./Ms. Smit) when mentioning a character. To achieve more engagement from the participants, the case was adapted to describe a neighbors' quarrel between Mr./Ms. Jaspers, a student representing a student's house and his/her full time working neighbor Mr./Ms. Smit. In both synchronous conditions the participant always played the role of the student. In the e-mail condition the participants were randomly assigned to a role. In addition, the case was rewritten into an I-perspective and eight different versions of the case were made, which included al possible gender combinations between participants or between participant and confederate. The case consists of three parts. The first part describes a personalized chronological story in which the problems with the neighbor are explained. The second part first provides information about Smit's and Jasper's feelings about the conflict, this part is identical for both parties, and the third part provides personalized objectives and personalized accusations that could be made towards the other party. The case focuses on disagreements between conflicting parties regarding noise pollution, litter, a domesticated animal and privacy concerns. The case was similar for all conditions, however the last paragraph was slightly adapted to meet the specific media condition:

> *"The responsible City Council member suggested that you and Mr. Smit participated in a negotiation at a neutral location/an online chat negotiation/an e-mail negotiation."*

This resulted in three different cases, one for each condition, and eight versions because of the possible gender combinations in the dyads. The participants were not explicitly instructed to come to a solution at the end of the negotiation. However, to avoid hostile negotiations and deliberate obstruction of the negotiation process, the participants received the following instruction prior to the actual negotiation:

> *"You are now going to have a conversation with the other party. During the (online) negotiation you are also representing your two roommates. You feel very unhappy about the situation; it does not fit your lifestyle nor your believes about how to live with your fellow human*

beings. You would like to have 'normal' contact with your neighbour again. This is why you would like to solve the problems in the present conversation. However, you do want be proven right because you believe that you did nothing wrong."

A questionnaire was developed to measure understanding, perceived trust and outcome satisfaction. The latter variable is included in the questionnaire since the number of successful outcomes may not have reflected entirely the participants' satisfaction with the negotiated outcome. The questionnaire is based on Naquin and Paulson's Organizational Trust Inventory (OTI-SF) [23], who adjusted the scale for measurements in negotiation settings. The OTI-SF items measure the affective and cognitive dimensions of three components of trust; 'reliability', 'honesty' and 'good faith in the fulfillment of the counterpart's commitments'. In addition, items concerning the outcome satisfaction and the mutual understanding were included in the questionnaire. The questionnaire consists of 39 items. The outcome of the negotiation was assessed by a yes/no question (successful or not). All other questions consisted of 7-points Likert scales ranging from 'I completely disagree' to 'I completely agree' or 'not at all' and 'very well' as extremes. The questionnaire items can be categorized into five constructs: *Outcome satisfaction, Understanding, Being Understood, Trust and Being Trusted.*

The latter four constructs are subdivided into constructs measured before and after negotiation. In all media conditions, the participants had to indicate to what extent they understood and trusted the other negotiating party before the negotiation, based on the story and the description of the other party in the case. This indication provided a baseline to measure the possible changes in understanding and trust during a FtF, a chat and an e-mail negotiation. The reliability (Cronbach's alpha) was high for all constructs, ranging from .59 to .90 (see Table 1).

2.3 Procedure

The FtF negotiations took place in a small conference room and the online chat negotiations in the laboratory facilities, both at the Tilburg University Campus. Upon arrival, the participants were asked to fill in a consent form. Then, they were asked to read the case and to prepare their specific role. In both synchronous conditions, the participants played the role of the student. A confederate played the role of the neighbor. While reading the case the participant and the confederate were placed in different rooms. During the whole experiment the notion that the confederate was also a student participant was upheld. In the FtF condition the participant and the confederate were placed together in the conference room after having prepared the case. They were introduced to each other and were asked to take place (the seats were marked with name tags). Final instructions were given right before the negotiation including a quick recap of the case; "You want to achieve your goals, but you also want to have a good relationship with your neighbor" and instructions to walk out of the room when the negotiation was finished. The experiment leader turned on the camera in order to record the interaction process and left the room. In the online chat condition the participants were placed in an individual computer cabin and were given the same instructions, including extra instructions about the usage of the interface. The participant and the

Table 1. The reliability of the constructs used as dependent variable (Cronbach's Alpha).

Construct	α	Nr. of items	Example items
Outcome satisfaction	.59	5	I am satisfied with the outcome
Understanding			
Before negotiation	.76	4	To what extent did you understand the other party?
After negotiation	.74	4	How well did you understand the needs of the other party?
Being understood			
Before negotiation	.84	3	To what extent did the other party understand you?
After negotiation	.90	3	How well did the other party understand your needs?
Trust			
Before negotiation	.88	3	How well did you trust the other party?
After negotiation	.90	3	To what extent do you think the other party was honest?
Being trusted			
Before negotiation	.88	3	How well did the other party trust you?
After negotiation	.90	3	To what extent did the other party think you were honest?

confederate did not see each other before or during the experiment. After the negotiation, the participants had to fill out the questionnaire on trust and understanding.

To determine the amount of time needed for the synchronous chat experiments, previous research was consulted regarding the difference between FtF communication and synchronous computer-mediated communication. Studies report allowing online participants a communication time span four times the amount of time provided for FtF participants [24], twice the amount of time [25] or even studies that provided participants in both conditions with an equal amount of time [26, 27]. However, since the study of Siegel [28] showed that typing and reading are physically more time consuming than speaking and listening and that typing accounted for the difference in number of remarks generated by participants in FtF and computer-mediated communication, the participants in this study were granted more time in the online condition than in the FtF condition. For the total experiment, including reading the case and answering the questionnaire, 60 min were scheduled in the FtF condition with a maximum negotiation length of 35 min. For the online condition a small pre-study was performed to examine whether the amount of 70 min, with a maximum negotiation lengths of 45 min was sufficient. The pre-study showed that the negotiation had to be prorogued during the final bargaining moments. Therefore, the time was adjusted to 90 min for the total experiment, with a maximum negotiation length of 55 min.

Since the e-mail negotiations are asynchronous and therefore more time consuming, the procedure was different from the other conditions. The experiment consisted of two parties negotiating by e-mail. To secure the a-synchronicity of the experiments the participants were given a maximum of seven days to complete the negotiation. The consent form, the case description and the further instructions for the negotiation were given face-to-face during a meeting at Tilburg University where the participants would be randomly assigned to either the role of 'Jaspers' or the role of 'Smit'. After reading the case, the participants were asked to fill out the pre-negotiation questionnaire on understanding and trust. Then, they received further instructions; to prevent premature abandon from the experiment, the participants were instructed that they would receive a total of two course credit points after completing the whole experiment. At that point they were also briefed that the experiment would be finished after the post-negotiation questionnaire was filled out. The participants would receive the questionnaire after indicating in the negotiation interface that they reached a solution. When the negotiation was unsuccessful, the participants would receive the questionnaire after expiration of the deadline (day 7 of the negotiation).

For both online negotiation conditions an online interface was developed that allowed the participants to either chat synchronously or to send e-mails. The interfaces for both conditions were similar. The environment was designed to only show the messages that were send and received without any further distractions.

3   Results

In the synchronous conditions the participants negotiated with a confederate, therefore within each dyad only the participant answered the questionnaire and those data have been used for further analyses. In the e-mail condition the dyads consisted of two participants who both filled out the questionnaire. Within that condition, the mean of both participants is calculated as the dyad-mean, which has been used in the further analyses.

First, the negotiation outcomes were analyzed. The participants seemed to perform equally well in all conditions: in the FtF negotiations 18 of the 19 participants (94.7 %) reached an agreement, in the chat negotiations 17 out of the 20 participants (85.0 %) reached an agreement and in the e-mail negotiations 15 out of 18 dyads reached an agreement (83.3%). In addition, the participants' satisfaction with the negotiated outcome was analyzed by conducting an ANOVA [29]. There was no significant difference between the communication mode conditions for Outcome Satisfaction, $F(2, 54) = 0.14$, $p = .87$, indicating that the results obtained in the FtF negotiations ($M = 4.56$, $SD = 0.89$), the chat negotiations ($M = 4.52$, $SD = 0.66$) and the e-mail negotiations ($M = 4.44$, $SD = 0.45$) were equally satisfying for the participants.

Secondly, in order to study the effect of the communication mode on the negotiation process, repeated-measures ANOVA's [29] were conducted for each pre- and post measurement of the perception variables as a within subject factor and communication mode as the between-factor (see Table 2 for the means). A main effect was found for the process: all perception measures were significantly higher after the negotiation than before the negotiation (*Understanding the other* $F(1, 54) = 154.92$, $p < .001$, *Being*

Table 2. Means and standard deviation of trust and understanding in negotiations

Constructs	Face-to-face negotiation (N-dyad = 19) M (SD)		Online e-mail negotiation (N-dyad = 18) M (SD)		Online chat negotiation (N-dyad = 20) M (SD)	
	Before	After	Before	After	Before	After
Understanding	3.49 (1.14)	5.61 (0.50)	4.22 (0.61)	5.21 (0.49)	3.68 (0.89)	5.09 (0.88)
Being understood	1.98 (0.84)	4.79 (1.00)	2.27 (0.58)	4.23 (0.83)	2.60 (0.96)	4.20 (1.23)
Trust	2.56 (1.11)	5.09 (0.64)	3.06 (0.59)	4.43 (0.64)	2.70 (1.22)	4.38 (1.37)
Being trusted	2.35 (1.02)	4.86 (1.24)	2.64 (0.63)	4.56 (0.95)	2.80 (0.99)	4.82 (1.02)

understood $F(1, 54) = 150.72$, $p < .001$, *Trusting the other* $F(1, 54) = 98.71$, $p < .001$ and *Being Trusted* $F(1, 54) = 130.66$, $p < .001$). This indicates that the process of negotiation increased the feelings of mutual understanding and mutual trust.

Understanding the Other. The repeated-measures analyses also showed significant interaction effects between the perception variables and the communication mode, indicating that the increase of the variables was not equal for all communication modes. For *Understanding,* an interaction effect was found between communication mode and process: $F(1, 54) = 7.20$, $p < .005$. Pairwise comparison of the pre-negotiation understanding showed that participants felt more understanding for the other party before e-mail negotiations compared to FtF negotiations *(p = .02)* and chat negotiations *(p = .07)*. Understanding of the other party before a chat negotiation did not differ from FtF negotiations *(p = .51)*. The feelings of understanding the other changed during the negotiation since the pattern of post-understanding differed from pre-understanding. The understanding for the other party after a FtF negotiation is higher than after a chat negotiation *(p = .02)* and than after e-mail negotiation *(p = .07)*. E-mail and chat negotiations did not differ from each other in this respect *(p = .57)*. Figure 1 provides a plot of the pre- and post-negotiation understanding.

Being Understood. A significant interaction effect was also found between the pre- and post measurements and the communication mode on the feelings of *Being Understood* by the other party (F $(1, 54) = 4.35$, $p < .05$). Pairwise comparison of the communication modes showed that the feelings of being understood are significantly higher before a chat negotiation than before a FtF negotiation *(p = .02)*. No other significant differences between chat negotiation and e-mail negotiation *(p = .22)* or e-mail and FtF negotiations *(p = .30)* were found. The feelings of being understood by the other party after the negotiations show a similar pattern. After a FtF negotiation, the feelings of being understood are marginally higher than after a chat negotiation *(p = .08)*. No significant differences between chat negotiation and e-mail negotiation *(p = .93)* or e-mail and FtF negotiations *(p = .11)* were found. Figure 2 provides a plot of the pre- and post-negotiation understanding.

Trust and Being Trusted. The same interaction effect was found for *Trust* (F(1, 54) = 3.43, $p < .05$). Pairwise comparisons showed that there were no significant differences between the communication modes for the feelings of trust before the

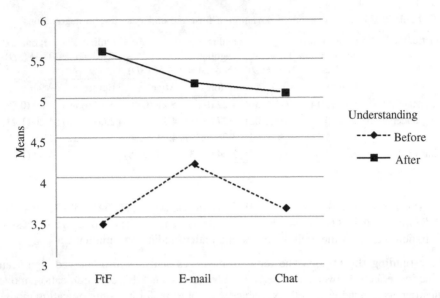

Fig. 1. Before and after measurements of the communication modes on understanding.

negotiation. After the negotiation the feelings of trust were significantly higher for FtF negotiations compared to chat negotiations *(p = .03)* and e-mail negotiations *(p = .04)*. Chat and e-mail did not differ *(p = .87)*. Figure 3 provides a plot of the pre- and post-negotiation Trust. Finally, no interaction effect for *Being Trusted* was found (F(1, 54) = 0.94, p = .40).

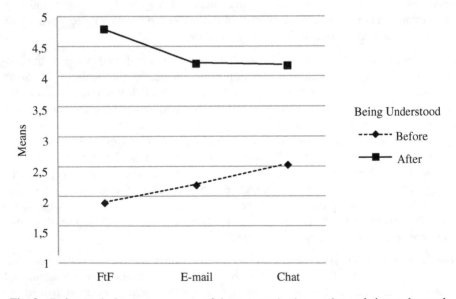

Fig. 2. Before and after measurements of the communication modes on being understood.

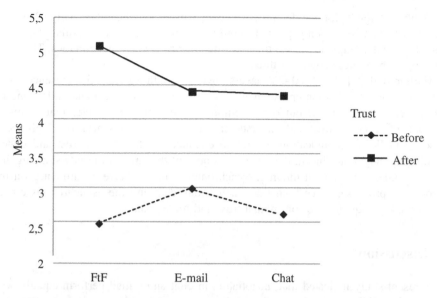

Fig. 3. Before and after measurements of the communication modes on trust.

4 Conclusion

The objective of this study was to unravel the effects of social presence and synchronicity on the creation of mutual trust and understanding in negotiations. When assessing the negotiations outcomes and the participants' satisfaction with the outcome, all three communication modes seem to yield equally successful negotiations. In addition, when considering the process, the mutual trust and understanding increased significantly in all communication modes. The participants in the e-mail conditions experienced higher understanding for the other party before the negotiation than FtF and chat participants and chat negotiators felt more understood by the other party before the negotiation than FtF negotiators. There were no differences on mutual trust. This indicates that the participant's awareness about the negotiation medium influences his/hers perception of the other party described in the case. However, these differences completely disappear during and after the negotiation.

The results of the post measurements confirmed the idea that indeed communicating face-to-face is more beneficial for understanding the other party than communicating by chat or e-mail negotiations since the feelings of being understood by the other party are significantly higher after a FtF negotiation than after a chat negotiation. However, no significant difference between FtF and e-mail negotiation was found. Also, Trust in the other party turned out to be higher after a FtF negotiation than after a chat or an e-mail negotiation. However, the communication mode had no effect on the feeling of how much the negotiator was trusted by the other. Summarized, negotiating FtF yielded higher Understanding for and Trust in the other party than chat and e-mail negotiations. However, the FtF and e-mail negotiations seemed to create similar feelings of being understood by the other party. Moreover, the communication modes show no difference for the feelings of being trusted by the other party. The first hypothesis is therefore only partially confirmed. In addition, the results show that mutual understanding and mutual trust are equal for both CMC negotiations. This does not support hypotheses two and three.

Earlier studies [11, 17, 20–22] have shown that both a rich social presence and a high synchronicity of communication are beneficial for mutual trust and understanding during negotiations. These outcomes demonstrate that the only factor that seems to have an influence on trust and understanding is the social presence. The high social presence in FtF communication seemed to enhance the feelings of trust and understanding the negotiator has in the other party but not the amount of understanding and trust the other party has in him/her. Synchronicity did not have an influence on the negotiation processes since both the synchronous chat and the asynchronous e-mail condition have equal scores on mutual trust and understanding.

5 Discussion

The present study indicated that, negotiators in chat and e-mail perform equally well compared to FtF negotiators, as far as the success rate in terms of agreement and negotiator's satisfaction is concerned. The level of trust and understanding increased in all medium conditions, although this was stronger in the FtF negotiations. However, when focusing on the post negotiation level of the trust and understanding variables, the picture is more nuanced. FtF negotiations still yield higher levels of trust and understanding for the counterpart but interestingly no difference arises for the experience of how well the negotiator was understood and trusted by the other. Building rapport in chat and e-mail negotiations seems therefore equally successful as in FtF-negotiations for the impression you think you make on the other party, but less successful for the impression you have of that counterpart. This differential effect of perspective is intriguing and gives rise to interesting interpretations. It may have to do with the role of non-verbal communication and the impact of the visual impression the counterpart makes. In chat and e-mail negotiations the level of trust and understanding the other party evokes is entirely based on the verbal communication as transmitted in the written messages. In FtF negotiations, visual impressions, prosodies and wordings of the message all contribute to the impression the negotiator makes. In other words, the online negotiator has less cues to convince the other of his trustworthiness and this may well have been at the basis of the lower level of trust in and understanding of the other. These findings seem to contradict the findings of Pesendorfer and Koeszegi [22] who concluded that counter-normative behavior and other escalating effects that can occur in CMC might be caused by the communication mode rather than by the ability of the medium to transmit social cues. In this study, the social presence of the medium is the most important factor for creating mutual trust and understanding. Synchronicity does not have an influence on the negotiation processes since both the synchronous chat and the asynchronous e-mail condition have equal scores on mutual trust and understanding.

Future research should focus on repeating this study with different computer-mediated conditions, for example an online chat with only a picture of the other party, online negotiation with only sound or only video, or a full videoconference negotiation. These different conditions can help determine the amount of richness that is needed to create enough social presence to influence the mutual trust and understanding similar to FtF negotiations. This might also determine what aspect of the high social presence FtF negotiation is the most important for mutual trust and understanding. In addition, in this study we conducted a simulation experiment to answer the research question. Although in two conditions the participants negotiated with a trained confederate, the negotiation in the academic environment may still be different from real life negotiations in which tangible targets are at stake. Therefore, it would be interesting to conduct a similar study in real-life negotiation situations.

References

1. Bains, G., Andrade, K., Gallant, M.M.: The potential for mediating disputes online (2013). http://www.cfcj-fcjc.org/sites/default/files/docs/hosted/17436-mediating_disputes_online.pdf
2. Silbey, S.S., Merry, S.E.: Mediator settlement strategies. Law policy **8**(1), 7–32 (1986)
3. Winslade, J., Monk, G., Cotter, A.: A narrative approach to the practice of mediation. Negot. J. **14**(1), 21–41 (1998)
4. Kydd, A.H.: When can mediators build trust? Am. Polit. Sci. Rev. **100**(3), 449–462 (2006)
5. Butler Jr., J.K.: Trust expectations, information sharing, climate of trust, and negotiation efficiency. Group Organ. Manage. **24**(2), 217–238 (1999)
6. Rosenoer, J., Armstrong, D., Gates, J.R.: Click with Trust. Free Press, New York (1999)
7. Keen, P., Ballance, C., Chan, S., Schrump, S.: Electronic Commerce Relationships: Trust by Design. Prentice Hall, Upper Saddle River (2000)
8. Deutsch, M.: Trust and suspicion. J. Conflict Resolut. **2**(4), 265–279 (1958)
9. Parks, C., Hulbert, L.: High and low trusters' responses to fear in a payoff matrix. J. Conflict Resolut. **39**(4), 718–730 (1995)
10. Duarte, D., Snyder, N.: Mastering virtual teams; strategies, tools, and techniques that suceed. Jossey-Bass, New York (1999)
11. Short, J., Williams, E., Christie, B.: The Social Psychology of Telecommunications. John Wiley & Sons, London (1976)
12. Kiesler, S., Sproull, L.: Group decision making and communication technology. Organ. Behav. Hum. Decis. Process. **52**, 96–123 (1992)
13. Alonzo, M., Aiken, M.: Flaming in electronic communication. Decis. Support Syst. **36**, 205–213 (2004)
14. Anderson, E.D., Ansfield, M.E., DePaulo, B.M.: Love's best habit: deception in the context of relationships. In: Philippot, P., Feldman, R., Coats, E. (eds.) The Social Context of Nonverbal Behavior: Studies in Emotion and Social Interaction, pp. 372–409. Cambridge University Press, New York (1999)
15. Valley, K.L., Moag, J., Bazerman, M.H.: A matter of trust: effects of communication on the efficiency and distribution of out-comes. J. Econ. Behav. Organ. **34**, 211–238 (1998)
16. Morris, M.W., Nadler, J., Kurtzberg, T., Thompson, L.: Schmooze or Lose: Social Friction and Lubrication in E-mail Negotiation. Northwestern Unviersity, Evanston (2000)
17. McGrath, J.E.: Time, interaction, and performance (TIP): a theory of groups. Small Group Res. **22**(2), 147–174 (1991)
18. Walther, J.B., Burgoon, J.K.: Relational communication in computer mediated interaction. Hum. Commun. Res. **19**(1), 50–88 (1992)

19. Katsh, E., Rifkin, J.: Online dispute resolution: resolving conflicts in cyberspace. Jossey-Bass, San Francisco (2001)
20. Spears, R., Lea, M.: Social influence and the influence of the social in computer-mediated communication. In: Context of computer-mediated communication, pp. 30–65. Harvester-Wheatsheaf, London (1992)
21. Thompson, L., Nadler, J.: Negotiating via information technology: theory and application. J. Soc. issues **58**(1), 109–124 (2002)
22. Pesendorfer, E.A., Koeszegi, S.T.: Hot versus cool behavioural styles in electronic negotiations: the impact of communication mode. Group Decis. Negot. **15**(2), 141–155 (2006)
23. Naquin, C.E., Paulson, G.D.: Online bargaining and interpersonal trust. J. Appl. Psychol. **88**, 113–120 (2003)
24. Tidwell, L.C., Walther, J.B.: Computer-mediated communication effects on disclosure, impressions, and interpersonal evaluations getting to know one another a bit at a time. Hum. Commun. Res. **28**(3), 317–348 (2002)
25. Antheunis, M.L., Valkenburg, P.M., Jochen, P.: Computer-mediated communication and interpersonal attraction: an experimental test of two explanatory hypotheses. Cyberpsychol. Behav. **10**(6), 831–835 (2007)
26. Coleman, L.H., Paternite, C.E., Sherman, R.C.: A reexamination of deindividuation in synchronous computer-mediated communication. Comput. Hum. Behav. **15**, 51–65 (1999)
27. Mallen, M.J., Day, S.X., Green, M.A.: Online versus face-to-face conversations: an examination of relational and discourse variables. Psychother. Theory Res. Pract. Train. **40**(1/2), 155–163 (2003)
28. Siegel, J., Dubrovsky, V., Kiesler, S., McGuire, T.W.: Group processes in computer-mediated communication. Organ. Behav. Hum. Decis. Process. **37**, 157–187 (1986)
29. Scheffé, H.: The Analysis of Variance. John Wiley & Sons, New York (1959)

Discovering Characteristics that Affect Process Control Flow

Pavlos Delias[1,2(✉)], Daniela Grigori[2], Mohamed Lamine Mouhoub[2],
and Alexis Tsoukias[2]

[1] Department of Accounting and Finance,
Eastern Macedonia and Thrace Institute of Technology, Kavala, Greece
pdelias@teikav.edu.gr
[2] LAMSADE, Université Paris Dauphine, Paris, France
{daniela.grigori,mohamed.mouhoub,
alexis.tsoukias}@dauphine.fr

Abstract. In flexible environments like healthcare and customer service, business processes are executed with high variability. Often, this is because cases' characteristics vary. However, it is difficult to correlate process flow with characteristics because characteristics may refer to different perspectives, their number can be real big or even because deep domain knowledge may be required to state hypotheses. The goal of this paper is to propose an effective exploratory tool for discovering the characteristics that are causing the process variation. To this end, we propose a process mining approach. First, we apply a clustering approach based on Latent Class Analysis to identify subtypes of related cases based on the case-wise process characteristics. Then, a process model is discovered for each cluster and through a model similarity step, we are able to recommend the characteristics that mostly diversify the flow. Finally, to validate our methodology, we applied it to both simulated and real datasets.

1 Introduction

A great value of Process Mining is in discovering the real process flows when there exists a lot of variability in the process execution, and the organization's assumed process models are hardly verified. This is a common situation in flexible environments like healthcare or customer service [1]. The next step that could add greater value to organizations is to reach perceptive conclusions about how this variability is related to process characteristics. As discussed in [2], if process flow variability can be pointedly attributed to characteristics, a great potential for process analysis is unleashed: we will be able to correlate the control flow to other perspectives (e.g. the organizational perspective, the data perspective etc.). This correlation will guide the analyst in exploring the discovered process models beyond the initial insights, resulting in a more effective guidance for process improvement and redesign.

Although correlating process characteristics to the model variants seems like the natural next step for process analysis, it is not a trivial task at all. A number of difficulties are acknowledged: (i) The characteristics may refer to different perspectives e.g. control-flow (e.g., is this a splitting point?); data-flow (e.g., is this an emergency

© Springer International Publishing Switzerland 2015
I. Linden et al. (Eds.): EWG-DSS 2014, LNBIP 221, pp. 51–63, 2015.
DOI: 10.1007/978-3-319-21536-5_5

case?); organizational (e.g., are these resources in the same team?) etc. (ii) The number of characteristics can be real big (iii) Characteristics may not be evident in the Log (thus, they must be derived) (iv) The metric to discriminate cases (i.e., the dependent variable) may not be clear to process owners / decision makers. Because of this kind of difficulties, using ad hoc approaches are prominent in the literature [3–6]. In practice, a less sophisticated yet intuitive way to deal with this problem is to use filtering and subsetting techniques, available in all process discovery software tools. Undeniably, this practice is more or less based on the intuition of the process analysts, as well as it requires deep domain knowledge.

The need to disentangle process analysis from the analysts' intuition has been early identified in [7], where a suite of Business Process Intelligence is proposed to extract knowledge about the factors that affect process performance. Authors of [8] have put forward those concepts in the process mining field. They use machine-learning techniques (Decision Trees) to analyze how data attributes influence the choices made during the process execution. Following this concept, authors of [2] propose a general framework about how process characteristics can be derived and correlated. In this paper, we built on the same concept of discovering the characteristics that affect the process control-flow, by adding an augmented potential to the analyst's toolkit.

In particular, we do not require from the end user (process analyst / owner) to formulate any a priori hypothesis. Our goal is to propose an effective exploratory tool for discovering the characteristics that are causing the process variation. The focus is on bringing out the appropriate descriptions and delivering an extra layer of information that will make process models easier to comprehend. To this end, we propose a multi-step methodology. At first, we apply a clustering approach to identify subtypes of cases based on the case-wise characteristics. Then, a process model is discovered for each cluster and through a model similarity step, we are able to recommend the characteristics that mostly diversify the flow. This is a process of transforming data into insights for making better decisions, thus a methodology for analytics, as INFORMS define them.

There are two major contributions following this approach: The first is that it allows the population profile, as expressed by cases' characteristics, to guide the knowledge extraction. This way, clusters are more intuitively related to business / market mentality, that tends to consider cases (e.g., customers) and not procedural behaviors. The second contribution is about delivering an exploratory tool. Since the methodology is able to exhibit the most informative features that control the flow, users can explore the process without needing to make any hypotheses.

2 Related Works

In flexible environments, where flow variability is expected, discovering a single model could seldom provide clear answers, since the generated models would be complex and confusing (the so-called spaghetti models). Clustering different behaviors, and discovering a process model per cluster has been early identified as an effective solution to improve process comprehensibility [9]. This approach is coined with the term trace clustering.

In [9] authors create a feature vector for each trace. That vector comprises the activities and the transitions between activities of the trace. Then they use the k-means algorithm to separate the control-flow behaviors. The same similarity criteria are also used in [10] to form a similarity matrix for traces. After applying a technique that relegates the most dissimilar traces, a spectral clustering method is applied to deliver clusters with more related behaviors. Song et al. [11] build further on the idea of feature vectors, since they allow a number of attributes (beyond the activities or the transitions) to create a profile for each trace. Then they provide a wide range of distance metrics (e.g., Euclidean distance, Jaccard distance etc.) that can be used with an also wide variety of ordinary clustering techniques (e.g., hierarchical agglomerative clustering, k-means, self-organized maps, etc.) to produce coherent clusters. The approach of [11] is the first approach that allows non-control-flow attributes to be considered.

Another way that trace clustering can be used is proposed by [12]. The goal in that work is to detect concept drift causes. Authors propose to use the generic edit distance to measure the similarity between traces so that a number of control-flow patterns can be created and exploited as features by feature vector clustering algorithms. However, the focus of that work is to discover control flow patterns, thus no correlations with features from other perspectives is considered. Moreover, in [13], authors capitalize on the benefits of an active learning approach to improve process discovery. They cluster traces, discover a model per cluster and next they combine the accuracy and complexity of the corresponding models to estimate the clustering quality. After a few iterations, they are capable to deliver clusters that perform near optimally with respect to these criteria (accuracy, complexity).

All the above trace-clustering approaches have been proved to be able to alleviate the spaghetti effect from discovered process models. However, as described in the previous paragraphs, most of the proposed techniques do not consider attributes of additional (besides the control-flow) perspectives. Even when they do (for instance, in [11]), just by clustering, it is not possible to tell what is the impact of these attributes to the behavior. To respond to this additional requirement, another category of techniques, using supervised approaches has been suggested.

A popular idea, first introduced in [7], is to treat the decision points of the process model as classification problems. The classes are the different decisions that can be made while decision trees algorithms are used to give prominence to factors that affect the branching decisions. Perhaps the most visible implementation of this idea in the field of Process Mining is the Decision Miner [8]. The same concept is also applied in [14], yet focusing just on the multi-choice workflow pattern [15] case. In [2], the same concept is generalized by proposing a generic framework according to which virtually any characteristics can be correlated (again through decision trees classification) to another one. Authors indeed recommend the automated creation of a number of related characteristics to be evaluated as affecting factors. Finally, in [16] case data analysis is performed by testing for the existence of particular correlations.

There are two important differences between this work and these approaches. First, it targets to explain the overall model variation (not only branching choices in the decision points or variation with respect to a particular characteristic). We are interested in detecting the reasons that cause the entire process models to be different, not just in a decision point analysis. Second, our work uses an essentially unsupervised approach to reach this goal. More specifically, we do not expect from the user to perceive what is the variable that discriminates cases, we do not ask from him to state any a priori hypothesis. In other words, the user does not need to enter any dependent variable during our algorithm.

3   Methodology

The proposed methodology is inspired from the active learning approach. Active learning systems are asking *queries* in the form of unlabeled instances to be labeled by an *oracle* while they struggle to apply effective query strategies to decide which instances are most informative [17]. In the proposed methodology, the instances are process models and the oracle is a model-similarity algorithm. In this case, the oracle does not label the instances, but it provides a metric about their pairwise dissimilarity, thus indicating the most dissimilar process models. Then, the learning occurs through classification trees that try to figure out why these clusters of cases correspond to so different process models.

The starting point is a heterogeneous population of cases. Heterogeneity is expressed across a number of characteristics. These characteristics are observed for the whole population and are case-wise features. The clustering goal is to provide a partition of the population into groups of homogeneous observations. Then, we discover a process model per cluster. Assuming that there exist characteristics accountable for the process flow differentiation, we expect the clusters' process models to be significantly different. To test this hypothesis, we follow a flipped approach: We find the process models that significantly differ, and we check the population of the corresponding clusters for differences in their characteristics distributions. Figure 1 illustrates the basic steps of the proposed approach.

One could argue that it is possible to check for differences in characteristics' distributions in clusters derived directly by a trace clustering technique. Although trace-clustering techniques are expected to deliver groups with different behaviors, they provide little (or they do not provide at all) information about how much different is the behavior among the clusters. Moreover, the clustering decision considers the flow elements (e.g., transitions) as well as the characteristics. Therefore, their output does not explain the role of characteristics in the behavior differentiation. A contribution of this work is that it detaches the similarities of cases' characteristics from the flow

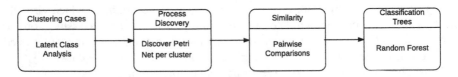

Fig. 1. A multi-step methodology.

variants. Such a detachment is provoked by the need to profile the population based on its characteristics and it is expected to support the discovery of the ones that affect mostly the process flow. To this end, the set of characteristics does not include any flow structures (set/patterns of activities). Similarity with respect to flow structures is evaluated during the sub-models similarity step (see Sect. 3.2).

3.1 Clustering to Discriminate Profiles

The first step of our methodology includes a case clustering, based on case-wise characteristics. In particular, we assume that some of the parameters of a postulated statistical model differ across unobserved subgroups. A discovered process model expresses the behavior of these subgroups. The models for all clusters form the categories of a categorical latent variable (it is called 'latent' because a case's class membership is not directly observed). Since during this stage we try to fit a model with non-standard distributional features, we propose to apply a finite mixture model to create the population subgroups. In particular, because our major concern is with the structures of cases (namely the latent taxonomic structure), we propose to apply Latent Class Analysis [18] as a tool for building the population typologies.

3.2 Process Models Similarity

In order to measure the similarity between two models, we use the notion of graph edit distance. The graph edit distance defines graph edit operations of the following kind: insert a new node or a new edge, delete a node or an edge, change a node or an edge label. Each operation e has assigned a certain cost $cost(e)$ and the graph edit distance is defined as the minimum cost of the sequence of edit operations which transform a graph into the other graph.

Process mining algorithms can discover models expressed as Petri nets. A *Petri Net PN* is a 3-tuple $PN = (P,T,F)$, where P and T are two sets of *places* and *transitions* respectively and $F \subseteq (P \times T) \cup (T \times P)$ is a set of arcs. For this work, a Petri-Net representation is mandatory, but the approach can be easily adapted to other notations.

In order to take into account the differences in control flow structure when calculating the distance, we transform each Petri Net into a graph (N, W, E) having two kinds of nodes, tasks N and gateways W, by applying the following rules: (a) the nodes set is equivalent to the transitions set ($N \equiv T$), (b) edges are created by replacing places having only one ingoing edge and one outgoing edge; the source and target transition will be connected with a direct link using a directed edge (c) for all patterns that form AND-splits, AND-joins, XOR-splits and XOR-joins, new nodes representing these gateways are inserted.

After parsing the two Petri-Nets PN_i and PN_j, we obtain two new graph models G_i and G_j respectively. These graph models are defined by the set of their elements, i.e. gateways, nodes and edges. The next step is to calculate the graph edit distance between the two graphs. We consider cost functions that assign constant values to the operation of insertion or deletion of nodes and edges. Let $0 < w_n \leq 1$, $0 < w_e \leq 1$ and $0 < w_g \leq 1$, be the cost of inserting or deleting nodes, inserting or deleting edges and inserting or deleting gateways, respectively.

There are two characteristics of mined process models that allow an efficient computation of their distance. The first characteristic is that the name of every task is unique within a single obtained process model. The second characteristic is that two tasks T_1 from the first graph and T_2 from the second graph can be seen as identical only if their names are equal. Edges are defined to be equal if they have identical sources and targets. Gateways are defined to be equal if they have the same type (splits, joins, etc.) and they have the same source and target nodes. Thus we can define the following sets: Nodes within N_1 but not within N_2: $N'_1 := N_1 \backslash N_2$ & Nodes within N_2 but not within N_1: $N'_2 := N_2 \backslash N_1$. In a similar way, we define the sets E'_1, E'_2 for edges and W'_1, W'_2 for gateways.

To calculate the graph edit distance between G_1 and G_2, we have to delete the nodes N'_1 because they are in N_1, but not in N_2. The number of edit operations is $|N'_1|$. We also have to delete edges E'_1 and gateways W'_1. Then we have to insert nodes N'_2, edges E'_2 and gateways W'_2. The total number of edit operations will be $|N'_1| + |N'_2| + |E'_1| + |E'_2| + |W'_1| + |W'_2|$.

Finally, based on the cost of these operations, in order to define a symmetrical and normalized value, the distance between two graphs is based on the fractions of unmatched elements (to be inserted/deleted) from the total number of elements (of both graphs) using the following formula:

$$\text{distance} = \frac{w_n * f_n + w_e * f_e + w_g * f_g}{w_n + w_e + w_g}$$

where f_n, f_e and f_g is the fraction of inserted and deleted nodes, edges and gateways respectively $(f_n = |N'_1| + |N'_2| / (|N_1| + |N_2|))$. This formula is adapted from [19, 20], where more general process models are considered.

3.3   Variable Selection with Classification Trees

After applying the model similarity algorithm of the previous section, we are able to identify the most dissimilar models. Then we can subset the dataset by keeping just the cases that are members of the population that correspond to those models. The clustering membership label can act the role of the dependent variable in a supervised learning approach (the characteristics will be the independent variables).

In this work, we propose to use a tree-based method. The basic reason that favored this choice is that non-experts more easily interpret tree-based methods. However, a drawback of trees is their accuracy level, since they suffer from high variance. Therefore, in order to create a more powerful model, we propose to use Random Forests (RF) [21]. The basic idea of Random Forests is that they grow a number of decision trees on bootstrapped training samples. During the creation of every tree, and every time a split is considered, a random set of characteristics (a.k.a. predictors) is used. There are a number of reasons why Random Forests are expected to deliver better results.

First of all, since the new dataset is only a subset, it is likely that the number of records it contains is small. RF are more suitable for this kind of problems (small number of records with respect to the number of predictors). Then, by considering different characteristics for every split, RF can deal with high-order interactions and correlated characteristics [22]. Moreover, through RF, it is possible to obtain a summary of the importance of each characteristic using the Gini index.

3.4   The Methodology Workflow

First, the initial event log should be pre-processed. A mandatory step is to construct a matrix whose rows will be the cases and columns the cases/ characteristics (unless such data are available as a distinct dataset). Then we need to determine the number of clusters that we expect to assign the cases to. In the proposed version, we select to choose the number of clusters that minimizes the Bayesian Information Criterion (BIC) of the clustering model. After we have selected the optimal number of Clusters, we solve the latent class model using [23] and derive the cluster membership of cases. This information is appended to both datasets (the event log and the cases matrix).

The next phase involves filtering the initial Event Log on the clustering membership, getting a sub-Log per cluster and discovering a Petri Net per sub-Log. Our algorithm is agnostic with respect to the discovery technique. Having obtained a set of Petri Nets (one per cluster), we apply the model similarity algorithm to get a measure of models dissimilarity. Such a measure allows us to focus on the factors that cause really significant differences in the process flow. The similarity metric is calculated pairwise for all the Petri Nets.

The algorithm proceeds by selecting the most dissimilar ones. Then, following a reverse logic, we move back to the clusters that produced these dissimilar graphs, and filter the dataset of characteristics (cases matrix) on only the cases that are members of these clusters. On the new, filtered dataset, we apply a decision tree technique treating the cluster membership as the dependent variable. Again, the decision tree technique to be applied is irrelevant for this algorithm, however we propose the techniques described in Sect. 3.2. Eventually, the leaf nodes of the decision tree are associated with the cluster membership, while the paths from the root to the leaves will be some classification rules.

We expect the classification rules to involve characteristics that have discriminative power with respect to the population (since they were used by the latent class analysis to create the profiles) as well as with respect to the process flow differentiation (since the compared classes (tree leaves) correspond to the maximal dissimilar models). Below, we present the pseudocode of the proposed algorithm.

```
Input: Event Log L
1:   Construct a cases / characteristics matrix C
# phase 1: Clustering
2:   Find optimal number of clusters N (BIC)
3:   Solve LCA for N clusters
4:   Append new column: Cluster_Membership to L & C
# phase 2: Discovery
5:   Subset L on Cluster_Membership: get L₁,…Lₙ sub-Logs
6:   For each Lᵢ: Discover a Petri Net PNᵢ
# phase 3: Similarity
8: For each pair PNᵢ, PNⱼ: Calculate models' similarity
9: Create a matrix with all pairwise models' similarities
10: Identify most dissimilar models M & M'
# phase 4: Classification Trees
11: Filter C on cases that correspond to M & M'
12: Apply Random Forest to C
13: Calculate variables' importance using Gini index
```

4 Evaluation

4.1 Simulated Data

In order to compare the proposed methodology with other approaches, we generated a benchmark process model and the corresponding event log for 1,000 cases using the PLG tool [24]. The parameters have been set to values that created a process model that allowed significant differentiation of the flows. Then we created 20 characteristics, in terms of categorical variables, like the following:

- 5 variables to significantly affect the flow. Every 'important' variable was connected with an XOR gate of the model, namely the level of such a variable affected the branching decision with a probability of 0.95 (5 % was allowed to noise, i.e., random assignment).
- 5 variables to averagely affect the flow. For 'quasi-important' variables the probability to affect the branching decision was set to 50 %.
- 5 random variables that follow a categorical distribution with a dominant level (50 % to 90 %) and two complementary levels that share the rest probability.
- 5 random variables that are uniformly distributed.

To check how characteristics affect the flow, we applied a number of trace clustering techniques, as implemented by ProM 5.2 (the Trace Clustering plugin). In particular, we applied the Agglomerative Hierarchical Clustering, the k-means and the EM algorithm using the Euclidean, the Jaccard and the Hamming distances. For all the techniques, we chose a standard number of clusters (5). Since trace clustering techniques do not provide a way to indicate the characteristics that affect the flow, we integrate trace clustering with the last phase of our methodology, namely classification trees using random forests. For each technique we noted down the top 5 most important

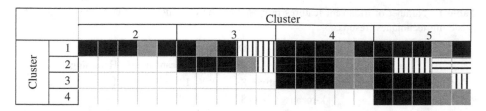

Fig. 2. Features that affect the flow, extracted from the k-means clustering using Euclidean distance dataset. The solid color signifies an important variable, the lighter color signifies a quasi-important variable, the vertical and horizontal lines correspond to random variables (uniformly and categorically distributed).

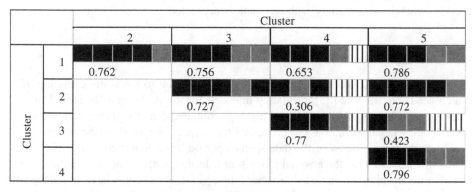

Fig. 3. Features that affect the flow according to the proposed methodology. The coloring scheme is the same with Fig. 2 and the numbers are the similarity distances between the process models that correspond to the clusters.

features, as indicated by the Gini index. Figure 2 illustrates the results for one of the most successful techniques, the k-means using the Euclidean distance, while Fig. 3 presents the pertinent results for the proposed methodology.

From the Table 1 and the Figures above we can see that the proposed methodology performs slightly better than trace clustering techniques (after augmenting them with the last phase of our approach). Nevertheless, the performance in terms of number of irrelevant features incorrectly identified is comparable (our approach is mistaken six times while there are a few other techniques that are mistaken eight). However, there are some elements in the proposed approach that yield added value. In particular, the added value is due to the models' similarity and the clustering components: The former allows to discover what features result in different (or similar) behavior (i.e., to distinguish the most informative ones) and to appreciate how different is the behavior among clusters. In addition, this component tabulates the models' differences (e.g., nodes inserted/deleted etc.). Another added value of our approach comes from the clustering component. Because it decides on grouping cases based on their non-control-flow characteristics, it delivers the (intrinsically homogeneous) profiles for each cluster. This is an important piece of information for process analysts and

Table 1. Number of irrelevant features proposed by the classification trees based on the trace clustering techniques' results.

		Distance metric		
		Euclidean	Jaccard index	Hamming
Clustering technique	Agglomerative	8	13	12
	k-means	8	8	8
	EM	9	8	8

stakeholders, when they want to explore the process variability from a case-wise perspective. These elements of added value will become more evident in the next section, wherein a case study with real data is presented.

4.2 An Application with Real Data

In order to assess the proposed methodology, we applied it to a real life event log of a Dutch academic hospital [25], originally intended for use in the first Business Process Intelligence Contest (BPIC 2011). This log contains data for 1143 patients of a Gynaecology department. We pre-processed the dataset like we describe below.

Since the time window of the data spans a period larger than two years, it is likely than some patients visit the hospital many times. In this work, if the same patient does not visit the hospital for one week, for her future visits, she is considered as a different case (this concept is also followed by [26]). Then, we eliminated cases that contain just one event. Moreover, each event may be related to many diagnosis and treatment codes. We consider each code to be a distinct variable. All variables of this kind are binary variables (true if that diagnosis/treatment code was noted, false otherwise). Next, the original dataset is an event log, but in our work, we care also about the case-wise characteristics. Therefore, if there is at least one event that is described as "urgent" during the case lifecycle, we describe the case as "urgent" as well. Finally, we exploit the different resources involved within a case to create two variables that indicate the starting department and the most frequently visited one. After pre-processing the data, we end up with a dataset containing 72 characteristics for 4640 cases that account for 147888 events.

The next step is to evaluate the optimal number of clusters. For this reason we used the Bayesian Information Criterion (BIC). More specifically, we solved the Latent Class Analysis model for different number of clusters (2 up to 10) and we selected the model that minimizes the BIC. In our case, 8 clusters yield the optimal BIC. Since every case is labeled with a cluster membership value, it is straightforward to copy this information to the original event log. The next step is to subset the log by the levels of the cluster membership variable. This will result in 8 sub-logs, each one corresponding to cases of a different cluster. For each sub-log, we discovered a Petri-Net by the ILP algorithm [27]. From the pairwise comparisons (illustrated in Fig. 4(a)), we perceive that patients belonging to clusters 2 and 8 have the most different behavior with respect to their flow in the process. The most interesting challenge now is to discover the

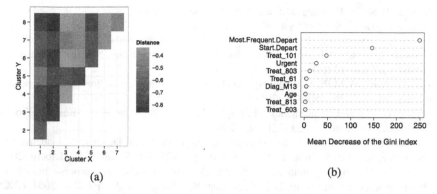

(a)   (b)

Fig. 4. (a) Pairwise similarities of the discovered Petri Nets. (b) The top-10 most important characteristics that discriminate cases of clusters 2 & 8.

reasons for this differentiation. Therefore, we return to the cases dataset and we filter it so that only cases of the two clusters remain. Following the technique presented in Sect. 3.3, we set the cluster membership as the dependent variable and we grow a Random Forest.

Figure 4(b) depicts the top-10 most important characteristics that influence the classification decision, therefore the ones that they affect flow variation. Actually, out of the 10 characteristics presented, just the first ones appear to play a role. These are the *Most Frequent Department*, the *Starting Department* and the *Treatment Code 101*.

The first conclusion that we can draw is that the single most important characteristics is the department that the patient is visiting. Although this seems trivial, there are some interesting insights that we can get. For instance, cases of cluster 2 are visiting most frequently the *Obstetrics & Gynaecology clinic* (with a 99.5 % frequency), while for the cluster 8 cases the most frequent departments are the *General Lab Clinical Chemistry* (63.4 %) and the *Nursing ward* (35.8 %). From that, we can infer for example, that we should check for pooling the resources of the *General Lab* and the *Nursing ward*; or that the *Obstetrics & Gynaecology clinic* is well separated from the other two departments and therefore some layout redesign could help.

References

1. Günther, C.W.: Process mining in flexible environments (2009). http://www.narcis.nl/publication/RecordID/oai:library.tue.nl:644335
2. De Leoni, M., van der Aalst, W.M., Dees, M.: A general framework for correlating business process characteristics. In: Sadiq, S., Soffer, P., Völzer, H. (eds.) BPM 2014. LNCS, vol. 8659, pp. 250–266. Springer, Heidelberg (2014)
3. Lakshmanan, G.T., Shamsi, D., Doganata, Y.N., Unuvar, M., Khalaf, R.: A markov prediction model for data-driven semi-structured business processes. Knowl. Inf. Syst. **42**(1), 97–126 (2013)

4. Ghattas, J., Soffer, P., Peleg, M.: Improving business process decision making based on past experience. Decis. Support Syst. **59**, 93–107 (2014)
5. Jarke, M., Mylopoulos, J., Quix, C., Rolland, C., Manolopoulos, Y., Mouratidis, H., Horkoff, J. (eds.): Advanced Information Systems Engineering. Springer International Publishing, Cham (2014)
6. van der Aalst, W.M.P., Schonenberg, M.H., Son, M.: Time prediction based on process mining. Inf. Syst. **36**, 450–475 (2011)
7. Grigori, D., Casati, F., Castellanos, M., Dayal, U., Sayal, M., Shan, M.-C.: Business Process Intelligence. Comput. Ind. **53**, 321–343 (2004)
8. Rozinat, A., van der Aalst, W.M.: Decision mining in ProM. In: Dustdar, S., Fiadeiro, J.L., Sheth, A.P. (eds.) BPM 2006. LNCS, vol. 4102, pp. 420–425. Springer, Heidelberg (2006)
9. Greco, G., Guzzo, A., Pontieri, L., Saccá, D.: Mining expressive process models by clustering workflow traces. In: Dai, H., Srikant, R., Zhang, C. (eds.) PAKDD 2004. LNCS (LNAI), vol. 3056, pp. 52–62. Springer, Heidelberg (2004)
10. Delias, P., Doumpos, M., Manolitzas, P., Grigoroudis, E., Matsatsinis, N.: Supporting healthcare management decisions via robust clustering of event logs. Knowl.-Based Syst. **84**, 203–213 (2015)
11. Song, M., Günther, C., van der Aalst, W.P.: Trace clustering in process mining. In: Ardagna, D., Mecella, M., Yang, J. (eds.) Business Process Management Workshops SE - 11, pp. 109–120. Springer, Berlin Heidelberg (2009)
12. Bose, R.C., van der Aalst, W.M.: Trace clustering based on conserved patterns: towards achieving better process models. In: Rinderle-Ma, S., Sadiq, S., Leymann, F. (eds.) BPM 2009. LNBIP, vol. 43, pp. 170–181. Springer, Heidelberg (2010)
13. De Weerdt, J., vanden Broucke, S., Vanthienen, J., Baesens, B.: Active Trace Clustering for Improved Process Discovery. IEEE Trans. Knowl. Data Eng. **25**, 2708–2720 (2013)
14. Sarno, R., Sari, P.L.I., Ginardi, H., Sunaryono, D., Mukhlash, I.: Decision mining for multi choice workflow patterns. In: 2013 International Conference on Computer, Control, Informatics and Its Applications (IC3INA), pp. 337–342. IEEE (2013)
15. Van der Aalst, W.M.P.: Workflow patterns. In: LIU, L., ÖZSU, M.T. (eds.) Handbook of Statistical Modeling for the Social and Behavioral Sciences SE - 6, pp. 311–359. Springer, US (2009)
16. Caron, F., Vanthienen, J., Vanhaecht, K., Limbergen, E.Van., De Weerdt, J., Baesens, B.: Monitoring care processes in the gynecologic oncology department. Comput. Biol. Med. **44**, 88–96 (2014)
17. Settles, B.: Active Learning. Synth. Lect. Artif. Intell. Mach. Learn. **6**, 1–114 (2012)
18. Clogg, C.: Latent Class Models. In: Arminger, G., Clogg, C., Sobel, M. (eds.) Handbook of Statistical Modeling for the Social and Behavioral Sciences SE - 6, pp. 311–359. Springer, US (1995)
19. Dijkman, R., Dumas, M., García-Bañuelos, L.: Graph matching algorithms for business process model similarity search. In: Dayal, U., Eder, J., Koehler, J., Reijers, H.A. (eds.) BPM 2009. LNCS, vol. 5701, pp. 48–63. Springer, Heidelberg (2009)
20. Gater, A., Grigori, D., Bouzeghoub, M.: A Graph-Based Approach for Semantic Process Model Discovery. In: Sakr, S., Pardede, E. (eds.) Graph Data Management: Techniques and Applications, pp. 438–462. {IGI} Global (2011)
21. Breiman, L.: Random Forests. Mach. Learn. **45**, 5–32 (2001)
22. Strobl, C., Boulesteix, A.-L., Kneib, T., Augustin, T., Zeileis, A.: Conditional variable importance for random forests. BMC Bioinf. **9**, 307 (2008)
23. Linzer, D.A., Lewis, J.B.: poLCA: an R package for polytomous variable latent class analysis. J. Stat. Softw. **42**, 1–29 (2011)

24. Burattin, A., Sperduti, A.: PLG: a framework for the generation of business process models and their execution logs. In: Muehlen, Mz, Su, J. (eds.) BPM 2010 Workshops. LNBIP, vol. 66, pp. 214–219. Springer, Heidelberg (2011)
25. Van Dongen, B.F.: Real-life event logs - Hospital log (2008). http://dx.doi.org/10.4121/uuid:d9769f3d-0ab0-4fb8-803b-0d1120ffcf54
26. Jagadeesh Chandra Bose, R.P., van der Aalst, W.M.P.: Analysis of patient treatment procedures. In: Daniel, F., Barkaoui, K., Dustdar, S. (eds.) Business Process Management Workshops, pp. 165–166. Springer, Heidelburg (2011)
27. Van der Werf, J.M.E.M., van Dongen, B.F., Hurkens, C.A.J., Serebrenik, A.: Process discovery using integer linear programming. Fundam. Informaticae **94**(3–4), 387–412 (2009)

Study on Temporal Change of Social Context: In the Case of Bicycle Riding Issue in Japan

Madoka Chosokabe[1]([⊠]), Hiroki Takeyoshi[2],
and Hiroyuki Sakakibara[3]

[1] Wakayama University, 930 Sakaedani, Wakayama 640-8510, Japan
madoka.chosokabe@gmail.com
[2] Oita Prefectural Government, Oita, Japan
[3] Yamaguchi University, 2-16-1 Tokiwadai, Ube, Yamaguchi 755-8611, Japan

Abstract. For decision making in a community, a set of alternatives needs to be identified. The set of alternatives should be consistent with recognition in a community (Social context). In this study, we define "social context" as typical wording in community. Such wording appears in newspaper articles. We focus on the issue of bicycle riding in Japan and clarify the change of social context by using newspaper article. We show that wording in newspaper articles on bicycle riding in Japan has been changed during the past 11 years.

Keywords: Social context · Newspaper articles · Text mining · Wording

1 Introduction

In the science of decision making, the effect of wording on people's behaviors is regarded as a framing effect. Levin et al. [1] presented some experimental examples of risky choice framing where the wording of the outcome categories could affect respondents' answers. Wording affects not only individual decisions, but also group decisions. Liberman et al. [2] have reported on the effects of the "name of the game" in a prisoner's dilemma experiment. For the half of the subjects, the authors described the game "the Wall Street Game". For the other half of the subjects, the authors described the game "the Community Game". Though the payoff structures of both games were identical, the names of the games affected subjects' choices. More than half of the subjects cooperated when playing the Community Game, whereas only one third of the subjects cooperated in the Wall Street Game. Ellingsen et al. [3] have conducted similar experiments in which the names of the games were "the Stock Market Game" and "the Community Game". Although they reported similar results, they also showed that the social framing effect vanished when the game was played sequentially. Based on their results, Ellingsen et al. [3] concluded that social frames were imbibed in people's beliefs rather than in their preferences. These literatures suggest that wording shared in a community can affect our decisions or beliefs.

The effect of wording is also important to make an alternative in participatory planning process in a community. Participants' ideas are summarized as needed and some of them are adopted to the alternatives in the process of planning. Their ideas are

© Springer International Publishing Switzerland 2015
I. Linden et al. (Eds.): EWG-DSS 2014, LNBIP 221, pp. 64–75, 2015.
DOI: 10.1007/978-3-319-21536-5_6

described by using language. The contents of the alternative are easy to understand, if participant's ideas are described by the appropriate wording which is broadly shared with other people. The contents of alternative probably are difficult to understand, however, if the wording used for the idea is different from the shared wording in a community. Our previous study [4] showed that adoption of participants' opinions is affected by the wording of these opinions. The wording shared in a community was called "social context" in the study. The newspaper articles were used to identify social context. When the wording of an opinion was similar to the wording typically used in newspaper articles, there was a strong possibility of the opinion being adopted to the alternative.

However, the wording shared in a community (social context) probably can be changed with time. The objectives of this study are to show the relationship between social context and policy decisions in a community and to show the change of social context. We focus on the issue of bicycle riding in Japan and analyze the wording in newspaper articles to clarify its change.

2 The Outline of the Problems

2.1 Our Approach

Figure 1 illustrates our basic model of community governance. The set of alternatives is constrained by the social context (I). A community chooses an alternative from the set (II) and subsequently implements it (III). The result of the implementation, in turn, affects the social context (IV). In this study, we focused on the framework wherein the set of alternatives was recognized by community members (I).

The set was not exogenously given in the actual community decision-making process. In other words, the set of alternatives was determined through the recognition of community members. When this recognition was altered, the set of alternatives could correspondingly be reorganized, and the final alternative selected could be changed. However, as alternatives were described by using language, recognition of community members was apparent in the specific wording used for describing alternatives. In other words, the wording used in a community constrains the way in which alternatives are described. When the typical wording in a community is altered, alternatives discussed in a community can also be changed.

This study especially defines "social context" as the wording used within a community and additionally defines it as the wording used in newspaper articles. Silverstone [5] stated that narratives within the media and those prevalent in our daily discourses are interdependent and allow us to frame and evaluate experiences. In the field of political science, it has been discussed that newspaper articles reflect community's recognition on issues [6, 7]. Based on their discussions, we assume that social context (typical wording in a community) appears in wording of newspaper articles.

As shown in Fig. 1, social context can be affected by the result of implementation of the past alternative (IV) and concerns in a community. If implementation resolved the problem, priority of the problem for a community may fall. In contrast, if community members recognize a newly emerged problem, social context can be altered.

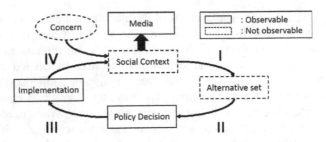

Fig. 1. Our basic model of community governance

In this study, temporal change of social context is observed through wording in media articles. By comparing the change with the decisions in a community, appropriateness of the model in Fig. 1 is examined.

2.2   Situation About the Bicycle Riding in Japan

Japanese society has not reached a consensus on the role of a bicycle in transportation. Some people use a bicycle as "vehicle," while the other people regard a bicycle as "substitute for walking" in Japan. The situation causes some problems. As far as a bicycle is regarded as a vehicle, a bicycle rider must keep to the left on roadway like a car driver. However, some people ride a bicycle on a sidewalk. As a result, pedestrians carry the risk of getting into a bicycle accident on sidewalk. Additionally, the environment for bicycle riding, such as the bicycle lane, has not been developed well. Another problem is illegally parking of a bicycle. At train stations, public space is often occupied by bicycles. Since some people consider a bicycle as substitute for walking, they do not hesitate to park their bicycle illegally.

3   Methodology

3.1   Data Collection

In 2.1, social context was defined as wording in newspaper articles, so we analyze newspaper articles by text mining to identify the social context. In the past studies, Mannarinia and Roccato [8] analyzed the uses of the term NIMBY ('not in my back yard') in the main Italian newspapers and showed that there were multiple and diverse descriptions about NIMBY conflicts. In the Italian press, the idea that the press supports traditional views of such conflicts is unfounded. Barboza et al. [9] applied ontology-based computational framework to the different newspaper articles in Buenos Aires and compared the positions that key political players occupy in discourse spaces that are modeled by two ideologically distant news media sources based on the same controversial public issue.

In order to identify the social context of bicycle riding in traffic policy, it is necessary to collect newspaper articles on bicycle riding in traffic policy. We use the database of newspaper articles in Japan named "Yomidas" [10] for collecting the articles in this study. This database is provided by Yomiuri journal in Japan. First, the articles including the two keywords "transportation" and "bicycle" were collected from newspaper articles in the year 2002, 2006, 2007 and 2012. In order to specify the articles on bicycle, only the articles whose title include "bicycle" were chosen for analysis.

3.2   Co-occurrence Analysis

In this study, wording is particularly defined as "co-occurrence" of words in the newspaper articles. Two types of analysis were conducted to analyze temporal change of the wording in newspaper articles. First we identified the related words with the keyword "bicycle", and then drew the network diagram of the co-occurring words. Both analytical methods are based on the concept of co-occurrence of words.

Co-occurrence of words is quantified by Jaccard coefficient in this study. Jaccard coefficient (Jaccard index) is used for comparing the similarity and the discrepancy of usage of words in text data [11]. It is one of the most popular direct similarity measures of co-occurrence data [12].

Jaccard coefficient of words A and B is defined as follows in this study.

$$J(A, B) = (\text{The number of sentences containing } A \text{ AND } B) / \left(\begin{array}{c} \text{The number of sentences} \\ \text{containing } A \text{ OR } B \end{array} \right) \quad (1)$$

Formula (1) shows how often the words A and B are used in the same sentences, which is the binary relations between words in the sentence. It is applied to the sentences on newspaper articles. If the Jaccard coefficient of words A and B is high, these two words tend to be used frequently in the same sentence on newspaper articles. Let X be a word. When J ("bicycle", X) is high, X is called the related word of "bicycle". It means that word X is often used with "bicycle" in the same sentences on newspaper articles. In other words, X is necessary word to represent "bicycle" on newspaper articles.

This study calculates the related words of "bicycle" on each article in 2002, 2006, 2007 and 2012 and observes the change of it. The related words have the potentials to reveal the situation of bicycle riding issue in each year and to show the change of the issue. As an example, we assume that J ("bicycle", X) was high in early period, then J ("bicycle", Y) has become high later. In such case, X represented the issue on bicycle in early period, and then the issue was shifted from X to Y.

The relationship of co-occurring words is also shown as network diagram. First, the sentences which include the word 'bicycle" are chosen for network diagram. Then two words with high Jaccard coefficient are connected with a link. In the following analysis, the top sixty pairs with the highest Jaccard coefficient are chosen for drawing links. In this study, related words and network diagrams of co-occurring words are detected by using KH Coder. KH Coder is the software for content analysis and text mining [13]. Unit for analysis is one word in Japanese, but some Japanese words are shown as two or more English words after translation.

3.3 Comparative Observation

For comparing social context (wording in newspaper articles) on bicycle with actual policy discussion, we focused on three agencies. The first is Ministry of Land, Infrastructure, Transport and Tourism (MLITT), the second is National Police Agency (NPA) and the third is Bicycle Usage Promotion Study Group (BUPSG). MLITT and NPA are the agencies of central government of Japan, and BUPSG is NGO. In order to describe societal changes of bicycle riding, we focus on the activities of these agents and marshal different elements of them.

4 Results

4.1 The Change of Related Words

Table 1 shows the number of collected articles and the number of sentences in each article. In 2002, for example, the number of articles including the words "bicycle" and "transportation" was 579, of which 106 articles included "bicycle" in their titles. These 106 articles consisted of 1208 sentences, of which 477 sentences included the word "bicycle". Jaccard coefficient was calculated by using 477 sentences to identify the related words with bicycle in 2002.

Table 2 shows the related words with "bicycle" in the newspaper articles and their Jaccard coefficients with "bicycle" in 2002, 2006, 2007 and 2012. The top 40 words with the highest Jaccard coefficient with "bicycle" are shown. The three words "transportation", "accident" and "safety" were common in each year. These three words suggest that there were many sentences about "bicycle accident" and "bicycle transportation safety" in the newspaper articles in each year.

There were some keywords which independently appeared in each year. For example, "station (No. 9)", "surround (No. 15)", "remove (No. 18)", "bicycle-parking area (No. 21)," "keeping (No. 36)" and "survey (No. 39)" appeared only in 2002. These words suggest "illegally-parked bicycle" problem. "Illegally-parked bicycle" means that people do not park bicycle in a parking area. They leave bicycle on the street or around railway station.

The word "illegally-parked" showed the second highest Jaccard coefficient with "bicycle" in 2002. However, its ranking had dropped to the 35th highest in 2007 and finally it did not appear in 2012. This result suggests that "illegally-parked" were often used with "bicycle" in the newspaper articles from 2002 to 2007, while the word

Table 1. The total number of articles and sentences analyzed in this paper.

	2002	2006	2007	2012
Articles including "traffic" and "bicycle"	579	672	647	842
Articles whose title including "bicycle"	106	175	165	292
-Total sentences	1208	1901	1709	3382
-Total sentences including "bicycle"	477	838	823	1586

Table 2. Related words with "bicycle" in 2002, 2006, 2007 and 2012.

	2002		2006		2007		2012	
N	Word	Jaccard	Word	Jaccard	Word	Jaccard	Word	Jaccard
1	transportation	0.202	transportation	0.243	accident	0.207	transportation	0.196
2	illegally-parked	0.175	accident	0.219	transportation	0.201	accident	0.195
3	accident	0.137	riding	0.171	safety	0.150	safety	0.126
4	safety	0.109	safety	0.135	riding	0.096	riding	0.119
5	ride	0.099	prefectural police	0.108	ride	0.095	use	0.113
6	use	0.088	ride	0.102	sidewalk	0.087	ride	0.096
7	walking	0.063	illegally-parked	0.089	walking	0.084	pass	0.077
8	road	0.062	breach	0.085	bicycling	0.080	road	0.073
9	station	0.060	use	0.076	prefectural police	0.076	sidewalk	0.073
10	counter measure	0.058	last year	0.071	manner	0.073	bicycling	0.069
11	held	0.057	walking	0.069	use	0.071	walking	0.069
12	many	0.056	in the prefecture	0.065	photo	0.060	rule	0.068
13	sidewalk	0.055	manner	0.062	pass	0.059	last year	0.068
14	last year	0.055	guidance	0.059	guidance	0.059	prefectural police	0.068
15	surround	0.055	many	0.053	in the prefecture	0.059	roadway	0.063
16	prefecture	0.049	rule	0.051	run	0.058	run	0.060
17	riding	0.049	held	0.050	rule	0.055	breach	0.049
18	remove	0.047	death	0.049	roadway	0.055	many	0.047
19	people	0.046	in the city	0.049	many	0.054	prefecture	0.046
20	commuting	0.046	road	0.047	last year	0.050	commute to school	0.046
21	bicycle-parking area	0.044	people	0.046	junior high-school student	0.049	in the prefecture	0.046
22	tournament	0.043	whole of country	0.046	in the city	0.049	manner	0.046
23	run	0.043	sidewalk	0.046	commute to school	0.048	car	0.041
24	in the ward	0.041	policing	0.046	road	0.047	guidance	0.038
25	development	0.041	counter measure	0.043	the station	0.045	people	0.037
26	conduct	0.039	pass	0.042	intersection	0.045	mobile	0.037
27	car	0.039	run	0.042	high-school student	0.042	phone	0.036
28	prevention	0.037	strengthening	0.041	conduct	0.041	development	0.036
29	bicycling	0.037	bad	0.040	lane	0.040	held	0.035
30	target	0.035	prefecture	0.038	whole of country	0.040	alert	0.034
31	prefectural police	0.035	intersection	0.038	increase	0.039	junior high-school student	0.034
32	children	0.034	automobile	0.037	alert	0.039	occur	0.034
33	whole of country	0.034	danger	0.036	children	0.038	brake	0.032
34	exclusive	0.033	this year	0.036	people	0.038	photo	0.032
35	association	0.033	front	0.035	illegally-parked	0.038	exclusive	0.032
36	keeping	0.033	junior high-school student	0.035	death	0.037	in the city	0.032
37	commute to school	0.033	elementary school student	0.034	association	0.037	set up	0.032
38	rule	0.033	commute to school	0.031	car	0.036	the station	0.031
39	survey	0.033	stop	0.030	prefecture	0.035	danger	0.030
40	railway	0.031	lamp	0.030	receive	0.034	city	0.030

became not to be used with "bicycle" in 2012. On the other hand, the word "roadway" had changed to be used with "bicycle" in the newspaper articles from 2007 to 2012 because the order of "roadway" had risen from being unranked in 2002 and 2006 to18th in 2007. Moreover it rose to 15th in 2012. The change of related words with "bicycle" suggests the changes of the topic about bicycle in the newspaper articles.

4.2   Co-occurrence Network

Figures 2 and 3 show the co-occurrence relationship of "bicycle" in 2002 and in 2012. The links of network represent the top 60 word pairs whose Jaccard coefficient were high in 477 sentences in 2002 or in 1586 sentences in 2012 (See Table 1).

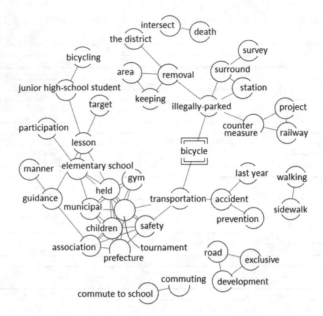

Fig. 2. Co-occurrence network of "bicycle" in 2002

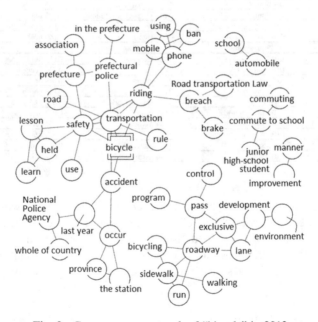

Fig. 3. Co-occurrence network of "bicycle" in 2012

As shown in Fig. 2 (2002), the word "bicycle" was connected with "transportation" and "illegally-parked." "Illegally-parked" was connected with "counter measure", "station", "surround" and "removal." It means that "illegally-parked" was often used with these words in the newspaper articles in 2002. The word group represents the issue on "illegally-parked bicycle" problem.

As shown in Fig. 3 (2012), "bicycle" was connected with "accident", "safety", "transportation" and "riding." "Riding" was connected with six words such as "bicycle", "transportation", "safety", "mobile", "phone" and "breach." The word group around "mobile phone" represents the topic of "the problem of using mobile phone while riding" in the newspaper articles in 2012.

In 2012, there was the word group including "roadway" and "sidewalk". The central word of the group was "roadway," which had six links. The connected words with "roadway" were "run", "sidewalk", "bicycling", "pass", "exclusive", and "lane". "Roadway" was used with these words in the newspaper articles in 2012. It suggests that the relationship between "sidewalk" and "roadway" became to be discussed in the newspaper articles in 2012. The issue on "development of bicycle lane on the roadway" was observed. These analytical results are summarized as follows.

- The word group including "illegally-parked" represented the context of "the illegally-parked bicycle" problem in 2002.
- The word group including "mobile phone" represented the context of "mobile phone use while riding" problem in 2012.
- The word group including "roadway" represented the context of "development of bicycle path" issue in 2012.
- The word group connected with "bicycle" have been changed from "illegally-parked" in 2002 to "bicycle riding" in 2012.

4.3 Activities for Bicycle Riding in Japan; MLITT, NPA and BUPSD

Table 3 shows the several major events on bicycle riding issue from 2000 to 2013. MLITT started the pilot programs in 2000, which promoted to decrease illegally-parked bicycle and developed parking area for bicycle and bicycle lane. This program had been conducted in 57 cities in Japan until 2006. MLITT set up a panel to discuss the future of bicycle riding in 2007 and also set up 98 model zones to develop a bicycle lane in 2008. Finally guideline of safety bicycle use was formulated in 2012. NPA has revised the Road Traffic Low. In 2008, the Road Traffic Law including bicycle riding had been revised. Under revised law, bicycle rider except such as disabled people need to use the roadway in principle. BUPSG was established in 2000 to diffuse the effective and safe use of bicycle riding. This group claims that both governmental agencies and municipalities need to change their policy from a comprehensive and cross-cutting perspective for safe bicycle riding. They proposed the legislation for promoting bicycle riding to diet members in 2002. They regularly hold a study meeting and encourage different parts of society to ride a bicycle safely. Especially they have strongly expressed that bicycle rider must keep to the left in a roadway.

Table 3. Major activities/events on bicycle

	MLITT	NPA	BUPSG (NPO)
2000	• Starts pilot program (∼ 06)		• Established
2001			• Annual report (01 ∼ 04)
2002			• Proposes the bill to Diet Members
2006		• Announces the toughening the law for drink-riding	
2007	• Sets up a panel		• Annual report
2008	• Sets up model zones	• Revises the Road Traffic Law	
2012	• Formulates a guideline		
2013		• Prohibits riding bicycle on the right in a roadway	

Figure 4 shows the ranking of related words with "bicycle" from 2002 to 2012 and the number of municipalities which settled on a plan for bicycle lane network. From 2002 to 2006, the word "illegally-parked" strongly co-occurred with "bicycle." Then the word "roadway" became to co-occur with "bicycle" more than "illegally-parked" from 2007. On the other hand, the number of municipalities which settled on a plan for bicycle lane network increased in 2011. It showed that municipalities began to recognize bicycle lane network plan as an alternative for transportation policy.

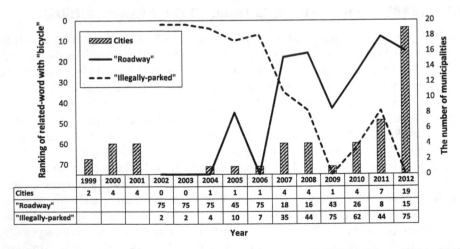

	1999	2000	2001	2002	2003	2004	2005	2006	2007	2008	2009	2010	2011	2012
Cities	2	4	4	0	0	1	1	1	4	4	1	4	7	19
"Roadway"				75	75	75	45	75	18	16	43	26	8	15
"Illegally-parked"				2	2	4	10	7	35	44	75	62	44	75

Fig. 4. The relationship between the ranking of related words with "bicycle" from 2002 to 2012 and the number of municipalities which settled on a plan for bicycle lane network from 1999 to 2012

5 Discussion

This study assumed that social context is represented as co-occurrence of words in the same sentences on newspaper articles. Co-occurring words with "bicycle" in newspaper articles have been changed during the past 11 years. The results in 4.1 showed that the related words with "bicycle" have been changed from 2002 to 2012. The word "illegally-parked" strongly co-occurred with "bicycle" in 2002 and 2006. However, it did not appear in 2007 and 2012 but the word "roadway" became to co-occur with "bicycle" in 2007 and 2012. High co-occurring words with "bicycle" probably represented the issue of bicycle riding on newspaper articles. The change of co-occurring words from "illegally-parked" to "roadway" suggested that the issue was shifted from the illegally-parked bicycle problem to the problem on the space for bicycle riding during the past 11 years.

The results of co-occurrence network in 4.2 also showed the change of the issues of bicycle riding. The word group including "illegally-parked" co-occurred with "bicycle" in the newspaper articles in 2002 (Fig. 2). The word group including "roadway" became to appear on network diagram in 2012 (Fig. 3).

From 2000 to 2006, MLITT conducted pilot program including illegally-parked bicycle problem. The word group including "roadway" and "lane" became to co-occur with "bicycle" from 2007. In 2007, MLITT set up a panel to discuss a safe bicycle riding and finally formulated a guideline for safe bicycle riding in 2012. The guideline included implementation of development of bicycle lane and informs the public of bicycle rule.

There was a time lag between the change of co-occurring words in the newspaper articles and municipalities' decisions (Fig. 4). Actually, MLITT had shown the development of bicycle path as is the case with illegally-parked problem at the pilot program in 2000. Nevertheless, the word "illegally-parked" strongly co-occurred with "bicycle" from in 2000 to in 2006. It suggested that the most important problem in bicycle issue was "illegally-parked bicycle" problem then for most communities. Some municipalities began to settle on bicycle lane network plan from 2011. The word "roadway" had begun to co-occur with bicycle since 2005 as shown in Fig. 4. These results suggested social recognition of bicycle issue had been changed from illegally-parked problem to development of the space for bicycle riding.

Our analytical results have some implications for how people generate alternatives in their communities. We need to consider social context in generating the set of alternatives. If the majority of members regard one concept as an alternative, the concept can be included. However, if the concept is not regarded as an alternative, it is excluded. In the case of this study, the concept of illegally-parked bicycle probably had been regarded by the majority in the early 2000's. If planners do not focus on the issue of illegally-parked bicycles in local transportation planning in 2002, there is a gap between the proposed plan by planners and social context in general public. This is because the issue of illegally-parked bicycle had higher social priority in 2002. This social context was observed from the co-occurring words in the newspaper articles in this study. On the other hand, when planners generates the alternatives in 2012, it would be better to focus on "the development of bicycle lane" and "the promotion of the rule of bicycle riding," because they have higher social priority in 2012 as shown co-occurring words.

Our analytical method is definitely not suitable for controversial issues, because arguments of each news media may be different. Also, our method cannot identify the detailed topics and opinions such as specific issues of bicycle riding because this method focuses only on terms on the sentences. In the actual planning process, the concerns of diverse members in the community should be considered in the process of generating various alternatives. This will require a small group discussion format such as a workshop (WS) in a community.

6 Conclusion

This study analyzed the newspaper articles and showed the change of the social context of bicycle riding issues from 2002 to 2012 in Japan. We defined the wording in a community as "co-occurrence" of words in the newspaper articles. Co-occurring words with "bicycle" were changed on the newspaper articles in the past 11 years. We also showed the relationship between co-occurring words with "bicycle" from 2002 to 2012 and the number of municipalities which settled on a plan for bicycle lane network from 1999 to 2012. The results suggested that social recognition of bicycle issue had been changed from illegally-parked problem to development of the space for bicycle riding. Furthermore, it is suggested that social context as wording in a community can be changed with time and municipalities' decisions can be affected by the change of social context. However, this method cannot identify the detailed discussion of the issue, for example, distinction between negative and positive opinion is not clear. Our future works are to reveal the relationship between wording and decision making and to establish the contribution to the decision making process.

References

1. Levin, I.P., Schneider, S.L., Gaeth, G.J.: All frames are not created equal: a typology and critical analysis of framing effects. Organ. Behav. Hum. Decis. Process. 76(2), 149–188 (1998)
2. Liberman, V., Samuels, S.M., Ross, L.: The name of the game: predictive power of reputations versus situational labels in determining prisoner's dilemma game moves. Pers. Soc. Psychol. Bull. 30(9), 1175–1185 (2004)
3. Ellingsen, T., Johannesson, M., Mollerstrom, J., Munkhammar, S.: Social framing effects: preferences or beliefs? Games Econ. Behav. 76(1), 117–130 (2012)
4. Chosokabe, M., Umeda, H., Sakakibara, H.: Comparative study of workshop discussions from the viewpoint of social context. In: Proceedings of the 2013 IEEE International Conference on Systems, Man and Cybernetics, pp. 310–322 (2013)
5. Silverstone, R.: Why Study the Media?. SAGE Publication, London (1999)
6. Prince, V.: Social identification and public opinion: effects of communicating group conflict. Am. Assoc. Public Opin. Res. 53(2), 197–224 (1989)

7. Brains, L.C., Wattenberg, P.M.: Campaign issue knowledge and salience: comparing reception from TV commercials, TV news and newspapers. Am. J. Polit. Sci. **40**(1), 172–193 (1996)
8. Mannarini, T., Roccato, M.: Uses of the term NIMBY in the Italian press: 1992–2008. Environ. Polit. **20**(6), 807–825 (2011)
9. An Barboza, F.C., Jeong. H., Kobayashi, K., Shiramatsu, S.: Ontology-based computational framework for analyzing public opinion framing in news media. In: Proceedings of the 2013 IEEE International Conference on Systems, Man and Cybernetics, pp. 2420– 2426 (2013)
10. Yomiuri Journal: YOMIURI ONLINE. http://www.yomiuri.co.jp/rekishikan/. (in Japanese)
11. Henning, C.: Cluster-wise assessment of cluster stability. Comput. Stat. Data Anal. **52**, 258–271 (2007)
12. Van Eck, N.J., Waltman, L.: How to normalize cooccurrence data? an analysis of some well-known similarity measures. J. Am. Soc. Inf. Sci. Technol. **60**(8), 1635–1651 (2009)
13. Higuchi, K.: KH Coder. http://khc.sourceforge.net/

Matrix Representation of a Basic Hierarchical Graph Model for Conflict Resolution

Shawei He[1,4], D. Marc Kilgour[1,2]([✉]), and Keith W. Hipel[1,3]

[1] Department of Systems Design Engineering, University of Waterloo,
Waterloo, ON N2L 3G1, Canada
s27he@uwaterloo.ca
[2] Department of Mathematics, Wilfrid Laurier University,
Waterloo, ON N2L 3C5, Canada
mkilgour@wlu.ca
[3] Centre for International Governance Innovation,
Waterloo, ON N2L 6C2, Canada
[4] College of Economics and Management, Nanjing University of Aeronautics
and Astronautics, 29 Yudao Street, Qinhuai District, Nanjing 210016, China
davinovo@163.com

Abstract. A basic hierarchical graph model for conflict resolution is proposed to handle a hierarchical conflict with two smaller conflicts as components. The hierarchical model can be represented in matrices and its stabilities calculated. This novel methodology is applied to water diversion conflicts in China, where the two subconflicts are caused by the construction of two local subprojects. Strategic analysis can provide decision makers (DMs) with a comprehensive understanding of a conflict and guidance for action. For basic hierarchical graph model, the matrix approach is an effective and convenient way to represent the model, calculate stability results, and predict equilibria.

Keywords: Graph model for conflict resolution · Hierarchical graph model · Matrix representation · Stability results · Water diversion conflicts in China

1 Introduction and Research Background

Conflict involves stakeholders with different interests and objectives. A strategic conflict contains two or more decision makers who determine an outcome by making independent choices [1].

The Graph Model for Conflict Resolution (GMCR) is an efficient methodology in modelling and analyzing strategic conflicts, and can provide stakeholders with strategic resolutions [2,3]. Compared with other conflict analysis methodologies, such as Game Theory [4], Metagame Analysis [5], Drama Theory [6], GMCR can handle irreversible moves, model common moves, and possess a flexible theoretical structure. It can model strategic conflicts occurring either currently or in the past and provide stakeholders with guidance for taking reasonable actions.

© Springer International Publishing Switzerland 2015
I. Linden et al. (Eds.): EWG-DSS 2014, LNBIP 221, pp. 76–88, 2015.
DOI: 10.1007/978-3-319-21536-5_7

A graph model contains decision makers (DMs), states, state transition controlled by each DM, and the preference relations for each DM over the states. Stability definitions describe how DMs interact with each other when a DM attempts to move to a more preferred situation. These stability definitions include Nash rationality (R) [7,8], sequential stability (SEQ) [9], general metarationality (GMR) [5], and symmetric metarationality (SMR) [5]. Stabilities differ in the foresights of the DMs and their perception of risks [3]. Equilibria in a graph model suggest resolutions for DMs as courses of action to follow. Other studies regarding the methodology of GMCR include coalition analysis [10–12], strength of preference [13], and the matrix representation of a conflict [14,15]. The solution concepts of a graph model can be described in matrices which are the functions of unilateral movements, improvements, and preferences for a focal DM and its opponents. Compared with the representation of a graph model in option form, matrix representation is a more efficient and convenient approach for calculating stability.

The graph model can be used to solve hierarchical conflicts. A common decision maker (CDM) is defined as a DM who can participate in each smaller conflict [16,20]. Other DMs are called local decision makers (LDMs), as each of them appears in only one subconflict. The theoretical framework of a basic hierarchical graph model has been established [20]. Theorems have been proposed to link the solution concepts in the hierarchical model with those in local models. However, the calculation for stability results in the hierarchical model are carried out according to these theorems, and are thus time consuming. Matrix representation is a more efficient approach for depicting the hierarchical conflict and facilitating the calculation for stability results. In this paper, the matrices representing the moves and preferences for each DM in the hierarchical model are constructed by those in local models. The algorithms for calculating stability results containing these matrices are constructed. These algorithms can be later incorporated into a decision support system (DSS). The matrix representation method is applied to the same example analyzed in [20]. The effectiveness of the new methodology is stressed by comparing it with the previous approach. The new method can save time in calculating stability results in the hierarchical model. The hierarchical model can provide DMs with an enhanced understanding of the interrelated conflicts, and guidance for taking beneficial actions.

In the rest of this paper, the theoretical structure for the basic hierarchical graph model is constructed in Sect. 2. The case study regarding water diversion conflict in China is given in Sect. 3. The comparisons between the new methodology and previous approaches are presented in Sect. 4. In Sect. 5, conclusions and contribution of this paper are given followed by the further work.

2 Theoretical Structure for the Basic Hierarchical Graph Model for Conflict Resolution

The theoretical structure of the basic hierarchical graph model is introduced. To represent the hierarchical model in matrices, the reachability matrices and preference matrices for CDM and LDMs are constructed respectively.

2.1   Structure of a Graph Model

A graph model for a strategic conflict is composed by a finite set of DMs, N, a finite set of states, S, and a preference relation on S for each DM $i \in N$. A move from one state to another for DM i is described by a directed arc, noted as $A_i \subseteq S \times S$. In a graph model, each state is represented by a node. Possible moves for a DM are expressed by directed arcs. The preference relation over S for a DM is defined [2,3].

The reachable list representing unilateral moves (UMs) for a DM i, denoted as $R_i(s) = \{s' \in S, (s, s') \in A_i\}$, can be defined by an $m \times m$ 0-1 matrix J_i [21,22] with the sth row s'^{th} column entry $J_i(s, s')$ written as:

$$J_i(s, s') = \begin{cases} 1 & if \ (s, s') \in A_i \\ 0 & otherwise \end{cases}$$

J_i is called a reachable matrix for DM i. The preference matrix P_i^+ for DM i represents the preference relation between any pair of states, which can be written as

$$P_i^+(s, s') = \begin{cases} 1 & if \ s' \succ_i s \\ 0 & if \ s' \precsim_i s \end{cases}$$

Note that $s' \precsim_i s$ means s' is less or equally preferred to s for DM i. The symbol $\precsim$ contains two relations between s' and s, which are less preferred ($\prec$) and equally preferred ($\sim$).

The unilateral improvement (UI) list from a state $s \in S$ for DM $i \in N$ is marked as $R_i^+(s) = \{s' \in R_i(s) : s' \succ_i s\}$. The UI matrix for DM i can be denoted as the Hadamard Product of J_i and P_i^+ [21,22]:

$$J_i^+ = J_i \circ P_i^+ \tag{1}$$

where "$\circ$" denotes the Hadamard Product, with $J_i^+(s, s') = J_i(s, s') \circ P_i^+(s, s')$.

2.2   Structure of a Basic Hierarchical Graph Model

A hierarchical graph model for a strategic conflict contains smaller graph models, called local graph models. These smaller graph models feature one or more common DMs (CDMs) who appear in each of the local graphs, shown in Fig. 1. DMs appearing only in one local graph are called local DMs (LDMs). The basic hierarchical graph model is defined as follows.

Definition 1 [20]: There are three DMs, consisting of CDM, LDM_1, and LDM_2, and two local graph models,

$$G_1 = \langle \{CDM, LDM_1\}, S_1, \{AC_1, AL_1\}, \{\succsim_{C_1}, \succsim_{L_1}\} \rangle$$

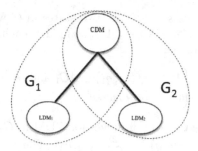

Fig. 1. Interactions of DMs in the basic hierarchical graph model

where $AC_1 \subseteq S_1 \times S_1$ and $AL_1 \subseteq S_1 \times S_1$ are arcs of move for CDM and LDM_1 respectively. $\succsim_{C_1}$ and $\succsim_{L_1}$ are preference relations on S_1 for CDM and LDM_1 respectively.

$$G_2 = \langle \{CDM, LDM_2\}, S_2, \{AC_2, AL_2\}, \{\succsim_{C_2}, \succsim_{L_2}\}\rangle$$

where $AC_2 \subseteq S_2 \times S_2$ and $AL_2 \subseteq S_2 \times S_2$ are arcs of move for CDM and LDM_1 respectively. $\succsim_{C_2}$ and $\succsim_{L_2}$ are preference relations on S_2.

Then $G = \langle \{CDM, LDM_1, LDM_2\}, S = S_1 \times S_2, \{AC, AL_1^u, AL_2^u\}, \{\succsim_C, \succsim_{L_1}^u,$ $\succsim_{L_2}^u\}\rangle$ is a *basic hierarchical graph model based on* G_1 *and* G_2, where AC, AL_1^u, and AL_2^u are arcs of moves for CDM, LDM_1, and LDM_2 separately; $\succsim_C$, $\succsim_{L_1}^u$, and $\succsim_{L_2}^u$ denote preference relations for CDM, LDM_1, and LDM_2 respectively.

The preference relation for CDM in G can be uniquely determined by comparing relative importance between local graphs [20].

2.3   Reachable Matrix

The reachable list for DMs in the basic hierarchical graph model can be expressed in matrices. The reachable matrices for DMs in a basic hierarchical graph model are integrated by the reachable matrices in the local graphs.

Theorem 1. Suppose $J_{CDM}^{(1)}$ is the $m \times m$ reachable matrix for CDM in G_1 and $J_{CDM}^{(2)}$ the $n \times n$ reachable matrix for CDM in G_2, I_n is an identity matrix of n scale, then the $mn \times mn$ hierarchical reachable matrix for CDM J_{CDM} in G is written as

$$J_{CDM} = \begin{pmatrix} J_{CDM}^{(2)} & \cdots & J_{CDM}^{(1)}(1,m)(I_n + J_{CDM}^{(2)}) \\ \vdots & \ddots & \vdots \\ J_{CDM}^{(1)}(m,1)(I_n + J_{CDM}^{(2)}) & \cdots & J_{CDM}^{(2)} \end{pmatrix} \qquad (2)$$

where $J_{CDM}^{(1)}(s_1, q_1)$ is an entry in $J_{CDM}^{(1)}$ ($s_1, q_1 = 1, ..., m$).

Proof. Suppose that states $s, q \in S$ are two states in G where $s = (s_1, s_2)$ and $q = (q_1, q_2)$ $(s_1, q_1 = 1, ..., m; s_2, q_2 = 1, ..., n)$. The reachable matrix J_{CDM} for CDM in G can be written as:

$$J_{CDM}(s, q) = \begin{cases} 1 & if\,(s_1, q_1) \in AC_1 \text{ and } (s_2, q_2) \in AC_2 \\ 0 & otherwise \end{cases}$$

where AC_1 and AC_2 are the sets of moves for CDM in G_1 and G_2 respectively.

(1) If $s_1 = q_1$, then $J_{CDM}(s, q) = J_{CDM}^{(2)}(s_2, q_2)$. The $n \times n$ diagonal blocks in J_{CDM} can be written as $J_{CDM}^{(2)}$.

(2) If $s_1 \neq q_1$, then

(2.1) if $s_2 = q_2$, then $J_{CDM}(s, q) = J_{CDM}^{(1)}(s_1, q_1)$

(2.2) if $s_2 \neq q_2$, then $J_{CDM}(s, q) = J_{CDM}^{(1)}(s_1, q_1) \cdot J_{CDM}^{(2)}(s_2, q_2)$.

(2.1) and (2.2) can be combined as $J_{CDM}(s, q) = J_{CDM}^{(1)}(s_1, q_1) \cdot [i_{s_2, q_2} + J_{CDM}^{(2)}(s_2, q_2)]$, where
If $s_2 = q_2$, $i_{s_2, q_2} = 0$; if $s_2 \neq q_2$, $i_{s_2, q_2} = 1$.

Thus, other $n \times n$ blocks where $s_1 \neq q_1$ can be written as $J_{CDM}^{(1)}(s_1, q_1)[I_n + J_{CDM}^{(2)}]$.

Overall, Theorem 1 is proved.   □

The reachable matrix for LDMs in the basic hierarchical graph model can also be obtained. The reachable matrix for the LDM in G is only determined by its reachable matrix in the local graph.

Theorem 2. Suppose that states $s, q \in S$ are two states in G where $s = (s_1, s_2)$ and $q = (q_1, q_2)$ $(s_1, q_1 = 1, ..., m; s_2, q_2 = 1, ..., n)$. Let J_{L_1} denote the $m \times m$ reachable matrix for LDM_1 in G_1 and J_{L_2} the $n \times n$ reachable matrix for LDM_2 in G_2, I_m and I_n represent identity matrices of m and n scales respectively, and $\otimes$ mean the Kronecker Product of two matrices, then the $mn \times mn$ hierarchical reachable matrices $J_{L_1}^u$ and $J_{L_2}^u$ for LDM_1 and LDM_2 are expressed as

$$J_{L_1}^u = J_{L_1} \bigotimes I_n = \begin{pmatrix} J_{L_1}(1,1)I_n & \cdots & J_{L_1}(1,m)I_n \\ \vdots & \ddots & \vdots \\ J_{L_1}(m,1)I_n & \cdots & J_{L_1}(m,m)I_n \end{pmatrix} \tag{3}$$

$$J_{L_2}^u = I_m \bigotimes J_{L_2} = \begin{pmatrix} J_{L_2} & & \\ & \ddots & \\ & & J_{L_2} \end{pmatrix} \tag{4}$$

□

The proofs from Theorems 2 to 5 are analogous to the proof of Theorem 1 and thus not demonstrated.

2.4 Preference Relation Matrix

To construct the preference matrices in the hierarchical model, a broad preference matrix for each DM in the local graph is defined. The preference matrices can be transformed from the broad preference matrices in the hierarchical model.

Definition 2. Recall that P_k^+ is a preference matrix for DM i in a graph model and $P_i^+(s, s')$ an entry of P_i^+, the broad preference matrix $\hat{P}_i^+$ for DM i is defined as

$$\hat{P}_i^+(s, s') = \begin{cases} 1 & \text{if } s' \succ_i s \\ -1 & \text{if } s' \prec_i s \\ 0 & \text{otherwise} \end{cases}$$

$\hat{P}_i^+$ can be transformed into preference matrix P_i^+ by

$$P_i^+(s, s') = \begin{cases} 1 & \text{if } \hat{P}_i^+(s, s') = 1 \\ 0 & \text{if } \hat{P}_i^+(s, s') = -1 \text{ and } 0 \end{cases}$$

The broad preference matrix for CDM in a basic hierarchical graph model can be determined.

Theorem 3. Suppose that states $s, q \in S$ are two states in G where $s = (s_1, s_2)$ and $q = (q_1, q_2)$ ($s_1, q_1 = 1, ..., m$; $s_2, q_2 = 1, ..., n$). Let $\hat{P}_{CDM}^{(1)+}$ denote the $m \times m$ broad preference matrix for CDM in G_1 and $\hat{P}_{CDM}^{(2)+}$ the $n \times n$ broad preference matrix for CDM in G_2. E_n is an $n \times n$ matrix with all entries 1 and I_n the identity matrix of n scale, then $mn \times mn$ broad preference matrix for CDM in G can be expressed as

$$\hat{P}_{CDM}^+ = \begin{pmatrix} \hat{P}_{CDM}^{(2)+} & \cdots & \hat{P}_{CDM}^{(1)+}(1, m) \otimes_p \hat{P}_{CDM}^{(2)+} \\ \vdots & \ddots & \vdots \\ \hat{P}_{CDM}^{(1)+}(m, 1) \otimes_p \hat{P}_{CDM}^{(2)+} & \cdots & \hat{P}_{CDM}^{(2)+} \end{pmatrix} \tag{5}$$

and

$$\hat{P}_{CDM}^{(1)+}(s_1, q_1) \otimes_p \hat{P}_{CDM}^{(2)+} = \begin{cases} \hat{P}_{CDM}^{(1)+}(s_1, q_1)E_n + \theta(s_1, q_1)\hat{P}_{CDM}^{(2)+} & G_1 > G_2 \\ \hat{P}_{CDM}^{(1)+}(s_1, q_1)\Theta + \hat{P}_{CDM}^{(2)+} & G_1 < G_2 \end{cases}$$

where $\hat{P}_{CDM}^{(1)+}(s_1, q_1)$ is the entry of $\hat{P}_{CDM}^{(1)+}$ ($s_1, q_1 = 1, ..., m$); $\theta(s_1, q_1)$ is a parameter with

$$\theta(s_1, q_1) = \begin{cases} 1 & s_1 \sim q_1 \\ 0 & s_1 \succ q_1 \text{ or } s_1 \prec q_1 \end{cases}$$

and Θ is an n scale matrix with its entries

$$\Theta(s_2, q_2) = \begin{cases} 1 & s_2 \sim q_2 \text{ or } s_2 = q_2 \\ 0 & otherwise \end{cases}$$

for $s_2, q_2 = 1, ..., n$.   □

Theorem 4. Suppose $\hat{P}_{L_1}^+$ is the $m \times m$ broad preference matrix for LDM_1 in G_1 and $\hat{P}_{L_2}^+$ the broad preference matrix for LDM_2 in G_2. E_m and E_n are m and N scale matrices separately with all entries being 1. $\otimes$ is the Kronecker Product of the two matrices. The mn scale broad preference matrices $\hat{P}_{L_1}^{u+}$ and $\hat{P}_{L_2}^{u+}$ for LDM_1 and LDM_2 can be denoted respectively

$$\hat{P}_{L_1}^{u+} = \hat{P}_{L_1}^+ \bigotimes E_n \tag{6}$$

$$\hat{P}_{L_2}^{u+} = E_m \bigotimes \hat{P}_{L_2}^+ \tag{7}$$

$\square$

The UI matrix for CDM and LDMs can also be concluded. The UI matrix for LDMs can be easily obtained according to Eq. 1 and thus not presented.

Theorem 5. Recall that states $s, q \in S$ are two states in G where $s = (s_1, s_2)$ and $q = (q_1, q_2)$ $(s_1, q_1 = 1, ..., m; s_2, q_2 = 1, ..., n)$. Let $J_{CDM}^{(1)+}$ denote the $m \times m$ UI matrix for CDM in G_1 and $J_{CDM}^{(2)+}$ the $n \times n$ UI matrix for CDM in G_2. I_n is the identity matrix of n scale, then $mn \times mn$ UI matrix for CDM in G can be written as

$$J_{CDM}^+ = \begin{pmatrix} J_{CDM}^{(2)+} & \cdots & J_{CDM}^{(1)+}(1,m) \otimes_v J_{CDM}^{(2)+} \\ \vdots & \ddots & \vdots \\ J_{CDM}^{(1)+}(m,1) \otimes_v J_{CDM}^{(2)+} & \cdots & J_{CDM}^{(2)+} \end{pmatrix} \tag{8}$$

where

$$J_{CDM}^{(1)+}(s_1, q_1) \otimes_v J_{CDM}^{(2)+} = \begin{cases} J_{CDM}^{(1)+}(s_1, q_1)[J_{CDM}^{(2)+} + I_n] + \theta(s_1, q_1)J_{CDM}^{(2)+} & G_1 > G_2 \\ J_{CDM}^{(1)+}(s_1, q_1)\Theta + J_{CDM}(s_1, q_1)J_{CDM}^{(2)+} & G_1 < G_2 \end{cases}$$

where $J_{CDM}^{(1)+}(s_1, q_1)$ is the entry of $J_{CDM}^{(1)+}$ $(s_1, q_1 = 1, ..., m)$; $\theta(s_1, q_1)$ is a parameter with

$$\theta(s_1, q_1) = \begin{cases} 1 & s_1 \sim q_1 \\ 0 & s_1 \succ q_1 \ or \ s_1 \prec q_1 \end{cases}$$

and Θ is an n scale matrix with its entries

$$\Theta(s_2, q_2) = \begin{cases} 1 & s_2 \sim q_2 \ or \ s_2 = q_2 \\ 0 & otherwise \end{cases}$$

for $s_2, q_2 = 1, ..., n$.

$\square$

2.5 Matrix Representation of Solution Concepts for the Basic Hierarchcial Graph Model

In a graph model with multiple DMs, the four solution concepts are represented in matrices [22]. As a basic hierarchical graph model can be considered as an overall graph model according to Definition 1, the solution concepts in the basic hierarchical graph model can be expressed analogously.

Theorem 6. (Nash) In a basic hierarchical graph model G consisting of G_1 and G_2, a state $s \in S$ is Nash stable for CDM, iff $e_s^T \cdot J_{CDM}^+ = \overrightarrow{0}^T$, where T denotes the transpose of matrix. The state s is Nash stable for LDM_1 iff $e_s^T \cdot J_{L_1}^{u+} = \overrightarrow{0}^T$.

$\square$

Theorem 7. (SEQ) A state $s \in S$ in G is sequentially stable for CDM, iff $M_{CDM}^{SEQ}(s,s) = 0$, where

$$M_{CDM}^{SEQ} = J_{CDM}^+ \cdot \{E - sign[M_L^+ \cdot (P_{CDM}^{-,=})^T]\}, \text{ and } M_L^+ = J_{L_1}^{u+} \bigvee J_{L_2}^{u+}.$$

State s is sequentially stable for LDM_1 iff $M_{L_1}^{SEQ^u}(s,s) = 0$, where

$$M_{L_1}^{SEQ^u} = J_{L_1}^{u+} \cdot \{E - sign[M_{N-L_1}^+ \cdot (P_{CDM}^{-,=})^T]\} \text{ and } M_{N-L_1}^+ = J_{CDM}^+ \bigvee J_{L_2}^{u+}.$$

The operator "$\bigvee$" is defined as:

if $M_1, M_2, ..., M_l$ are all $h \times h$ matrices, then $\bigvee_{p=1}^l M_p$ is the $h \times h$ matrix with (s, s') entry

$$ind\left(\sum_{p=1}^l M_p(s, s')\right),$$

when

$$ind(x) = \begin{cases} 1 & \text{if } x > 0 \\ 0 & \text{if } x = 0 \end{cases} \tag{9}$$

$\square$

Theorem 8. (GMR) A state $s \in S$ in G is general metarational for CDM, iff $M_{CDM}^{GMR}(s,s) = 0$, where

$$M_{CDM}^{GMR} = J_{CDM}^+ \cdot \{E - sign[M_L \cdot (P_{CDM}^{-,=})^T]\}, \text{ and } M_L = J_{L_1}^u \bigvee J_{L_2}^u.$$

State s is general metarational for LDM_1 iff $M_{L_1}^{GMR^u}(s,s) = 0$, where

$$M_{L_1}^{GMR^u} = J_{L_1}^{u+} \cdot \{E - sign[(M_{N-L_1} \cdot (P_{CDM}^{-,=})^T]\} \text{ and } M_{N-L_1} = J_{CDM} \bigvee J_{L_2}^u. \quad \square$$

Theorem 9. (SMR) A state $s \in S$ in G is symmetric metarational for CDM, iff $M_{CDM}^{SMR}(s,s) = 0$, where

$M_{CDM}^{SMR} = J_{CDM}^{+} \cdot [E - sign(M_L \cdot W_{CDM})]$, and $W_{CDM} = (P_{CDM}^{-,=})^T \circ [E - sign(J_{CDM} \cdot (P_{CDM}^{+})^T)]$.

State s is symmetric metarational for LDM_1 iff $M_{L_1}^{SMR^u}(s,s) = 0$, where

$M_{L_1}^{SMR} = J_{L_1}^{+} \cdot [E - sign(M_{N-L_1} \cdot W_{L_1})]$, and $W_{L_1} = (P_{L_1}^{-,=})^T \circ [E - sign(J_{L_1}^{u} \cdot (P_{L_1}^{u+})^T)]$.
□

3   Case Study: Water Diversion Conflicts in China

The South-North Water Diversion Project (SNWDP) is carried out on three locations, which constitute the eastern, the central, and the western projects [17–19]. As the eastern project is complete, conflicts are arising on the central and western route and will affect the construction of these projects. The background of these conflicts are discussed in [20]. Hence, these water diversion conflicts are modelled by a basic hierarchical graph model, and the stability results are calculated using matrices.

3.1   Modelling of the Water Diversion Conflicts in China

Local residents (LRs) and Chinese Government (CG) are the two DMs in the central route conflict. Neighboring Countries (NCs) and Chinese Government (CG) are the two DMs in the western conflict. The implementation of SNWDP will affect the interests of stakeholders along each route. The homeland for LRs on the central route will be inundated for reservoirs according to the construction plan. Thus, LRs are forced to be relocated. The construction of the western project on the Tibet Plateau can affect the water flows in the NCs such as India and Bangladesh. CG is CDM in the hierarchical model because it appears in both the central and the western conflicts. The two conflicts are considered as G_1 and G_2, and the entire conflict is modelled as G. As the western plan is still under discussion, CG considers the central conflict more important, denoted as $G_1 > G_2$. The options and states for DMs in each subconflict are provided in Tables 1 and 2. Detailed explanations on each option and state can be found in [20].

The reachable and preference matrices for each DM in two subgraphs can be obtained. Note that the row and the column of each matrix are labelled with the states shown in Tables 1 and 2. In a reachable matrix, the starting states are labelled in the row and the column of the matrix indicates all states that the focal DM can reach in one UM.

Table 1. DMs, their options, and states in the central conflict

DM	Option				
CG:	Full Central	Y	Y	N	N
LRs:	Agree	Y	N	Y	N
	States	1	2	3	4

Table 2. DMs, their options, and states in the western conflict

DM	Option				
CG:	Resume Western	Y	Y	N	N
NCs:	Consent	Y	N	Y	N
	States	5	6	7	8

$$
J_{CG}^{(1)} = \begin{matrix} 1 \\ 2 \\ 3 \\ 4 \end{matrix}\begin{pmatrix} 0 & 0 & 1 & 0 \\ 0 & 0 & 0 & 1 \\ 1 & 0 & 0 & 0 \\ 0 & 1 & 0 & 0 \end{pmatrix} \quad
J_{CG}^{(2)} = \begin{matrix} 5 \\ 6 \\ 7 \\ 8 \end{matrix}\begin{pmatrix} 0 & 0 & 1 & 0 \\ 0 & 0 & 0 & 1 \\ 1 & 0 & 0 & 0 \\ 0 & 1 & 0 & 0 \end{pmatrix} \quad
J_{L_1} = \begin{matrix} 1 \\ 2 \\ 3 \\ 4 \end{matrix}\begin{pmatrix} 0 & 1 & 0 & 0 \\ 1 & 0 & 0 & 0 \\ 0 & 0 & 0 & 1 \\ 0 & 0 & 1 & 0 \end{pmatrix} \quad
J_{L_2} = \begin{matrix} 5 \\ 6 \\ 7 \\ 8 \end{matrix}\begin{pmatrix} 0 & 1 & 0 & 0 \\ 1 & 0 & 0 & 0 \\ 0 & 0 & 0 & 1 \\ 0 & 0 & 1 & 0 \end{pmatrix}
$$

$$
\hat{P}_{CG}^{(1)+} = \begin{matrix} 1 \\ 2 \\ 3 \\ 4 \end{matrix}\begin{pmatrix} 0 & -1 & -1 & -1 \\ 1 & 0 & -1 & -1 \\ 1 & 1 & 0 & -1 \\ 1 & 1 & 1 & 0 \end{pmatrix} \quad
\hat{P}_{CG}^{(2)+} = \begin{matrix} 5 \\ 6 \\ 7 \\ 8 \end{matrix}\begin{pmatrix} 0 & -1 & -1 & -1 \\ 1 & 0 & 1 & -1 \\ 1 & -1 & 0 & -1 \\ 1 & 1 & 1 & 0 \end{pmatrix}
$$

$$
\hat{P}_{L_1}^{+} = \begin{matrix} 1 \\ 2 \\ 3 \\ 4 \end{matrix}\begin{pmatrix} 0 & 1 & 1 & 1 \\ -1 & 0 & 1 & 1 \\ -1 & -1 & 0 & -1 \\ -1 & -1 & 1 & 0 \end{pmatrix} \quad
\hat{P}_{L_2}^{+} = \begin{matrix} 5 \\ 6 \\ 7 \\ 8 \end{matrix}\begin{pmatrix} 0 & 1 & 1 & 1 \\ -1 & 0 & 1 & 1 \\ -1 & -1 & 0 & -1 \\ -1 & -1 & 1 & 0 \end{pmatrix}
$$

The hierarchical reachable, preference matrices, and UI matrices for each DM can be constructed accordingly.

3.2 Stability Results of the Water Diversion Conflicts in China

The stability results for the solution concepts in the overall conflict are calculated using Theorems from 6 to 9, as shown in Table 3. States in the hierarchical model are composed by the corresponding states in local graphs. For example, state (1, 5) contains the outcomes in state 1 in the central conflict and state 5 in the western conflict. States (2, 6) and (2, 7) are equilibria because both of them are stable for all DMs. As an actual outcome, state (2, 7) is sequentially stable for all DMs. At this state, CG is assertive in constructing the central project while compromising with NCs on the western project. The countermoves from LRs cannot sanction CG from implementing the central project. The stability results echo the analytical results calculated in [20].

Table 3. Stability results in the overall conflict

	Nash	SEQ	GMR	SMR
CG	(1, 5), (1, 6) (2, 5), (2, 6)	(1, 5), (1, 6), (2, 5) (2, 6), (1, 7), (2, 7) (1, 8)	(1, 5), (1, 6), (2, 5) (2, 6), (1, 7), (2, 7) (1, 8)	(1, 5), (1, 6), (2, 5) (2, 6), (1, 7), (2, 7) (1, 8)
LRs	(2, -), (3, -)	(2, -), (3, -), (4, -)	(2, -), (3, -), (4, -)	(2, -), (3, -), (4, -)
NCs	(-, 6), (-, 7)	(-, 6), (-, 7), (-, 8)	(-, 6), (-, 7), (-, 8)	(-, 6), (-, 7), (-, 8)
Overall	(2, 6)	(2, 6), (2, 7)	(2, 6), (2, 7)	(2, 6), (2, 7)

4   Comparative Analysis of the Matrix Representation Methodology

4.1   Comparison of the Matrix Representation Approach and Direct Calculation in the Hierarchical Model

The matrix representation approach can simplify the calculation of stability results in the basic hierarchical graph model. Earlier, this calculation was carried out using the theorems linking solution concepts in the hierarchical model with those in local graphs by He et al. [20]. In comparison, in the matrix representation approach, the reachable and preference matrices in local models are easily obtained. The corresponding matrices in the hierarchical model can be constructed according to Theorems 1 to 5. Stability results are then obtained by matrix computation, which can be performed by Matlab or MRSC, a DSS developed by Xu et al. [22]. Therefore, the matrix representation approach has simplified the calculation of stability results in the hierarchical graph model.

4.2   Comparison of the Stability Results in the Hierarchical Model and Those in Local Models

Compared with the results obtained in modelling each subconflict separately, the stability results calculated in the hierarchical graph model reflect a more comprehensive understanding of the interralated conflict. Thus, if the stability results in the hierarchical model are different from those in local models, the predictions of the model are reflecting its hierarchical structure. Taking state (1, 8) in the hierarchical model as an example, the two component states are Nash stable and unstable for CG in two local models respectively. State (1, 8), however, is sequentially stable for CG in the hierarchical model. At this state, CGs UI to state (1, 6) is sanctioned by LRs' subsequent UI to state (2, 6). Because CG regards the two subconflicts as interrelated and considers the central project more important, the Central Government will stay at the starting state for fear of the possible countermoves by LRs.

5 Conclusion and Further Study

The basic hierarchical graph model is represented in matrices to calculate stability results. The reachable, preference, and UI matrices in the hierarchical model are constructed. The matrix representation approach is applied to water diversion conflicts in China. The resolutions obtained in the illustrative example indicate that the priority on the central route for CG will result in the successful implementation of the central project. However, the western project should be suspended. The calculation in the example only requires the reachable and preference matrices in each local graph model as the input.

The main contribution of this paper is the design of a matrix representation algorithm for calculating stability results in the basic hierarchical model. This approach can be implemented using DSS, such as MRSC. Matrix calculations are faster compared with direct computation using the original approach [14].

In follow-up studies, the preference structure in the hierarchical graph model can be reconstructed. The importance of each local graph for CDM can be expressed by weights assigned by CDM according to its judgement. The basic hierarchical graph model can also be extended containing more local graphs. In addition, coalition among DMs in hierarchical graph model can also be studied by assuming cooperation among LDMs. It is possible to analyze whether their cooperation can result in outcomes that are beneficial to all of them, but this study is left for future research.

References

1. Li, K.W., Kilgour, D.M., Hipel, K.W.: Status quo analysis in the graph model for conflict resolution. J. Oper. Res. Soc. **56**(6), 699–707 (2005)
2. Kilgour, D.M., Hipel, K.W.: The graph model for conflict resolution: past, present, and future. Group Decis. Negot. **14**(6), 441–460 (2005)
3. Kilgour, D.M., Hipel, K.W.: Conflict analysis methods: the graph model for conflict resolution. In: Kilgou, D.M., Eden, C. (eds.) Handbook of Group Decision and Negotiation. Advances in Group Decision and Negotiation, p. 203. Springer, The Netherlands (2010)
4. Von Neumann, J., Morgenstern, O.B.: Theory of games and economic behavior, 1st edn. Princeton University Press, Princeton (1944)
5. Howard, N.: Paradoxes of Rationality: Theory of Metagames and Political Behavior. MIT Press, Cambridge (1971)
6. Howard, N.: Confrontation analysis: how to win operations other than war, Technical report, C4ISR (1999)
7. Nash, J.F.: Equilibrium points in n-person games. In: Proceedings of the national academy of sciences **36**(1), 48–49 (1950)
8. Nash, J.F.: Non-cooperative games. Annals Math. **54**(2), 286–295 (1951)
9. Fraser, N.M., Hipel, K.W.: Conflict Analysis: Models and Resolutions. North-Holland (1984)
10. Kilgour, D.M., Hipel, K.W., Fang, L., Peng, X.J.: Coalition analysis in group decision support. Group Decis. Negot. **10**(2), 159–175 (2001)
11. Inohara, T., Hipel, K.W.: Coalition analysis in the graph model for conflict resolution. Syst. Eng. **11**(4), 343–359 (2008)

12. Inohara, T., Hipel, K.W.: Interrelationships among noncooperative and coalition stability concepts. J. Syst. Sci. Syst. Eng. **17**(1), 1–9 (2008)
13. Hamouda, L., Kilgour, D.M., Hipel, K.W.: Strength of preference in the graph model for conflict resolution. Group Decis. Negot. **13**(5), 449–462 (2004)
14. Xu, H., Kilgour, D.M., Hipel, K.W.: Matrix representation and extension of coalition analysis in group decision support. Comput. Math. Appl. **60**(5), 1164–1176 (2010)
15. Xu, H., Kilgour, D.M., Hipel, K.W., Kemkes, G.: Using matrices to link conflict evolution and resolution in a graph model. Eur. J. Oper. Res. **207**(1), 318–329 (2010)
16. He, S., Hipel, K.W., Kilgour, D.M.: Water diversion conflicts in China: a hierarchical perspective. Water Resour. Manage **28**, 1823–1837 (2014)
17. Chen, Z., Wang, H., Qi, X.: Pricing and water resource allocation scheme for the south-to-north water diversion project in China. Water Resour. Manage **27**(5), 1457–1472 (2013)
18. Yang, H., Zehnder, A.J.: The south-north water transfer project in China: an analysis of water demand uncertainty and environmental objectives in decision making. Water Int. **30**(3), 339–349 (2005)
19. Berkoff, J.: China: the South-North water transfer project-is it justified? Water Policy **5**(1), 1–28 (2003)
20. He, S., Kilgour, D.M., Hipel, K.M.: A basic hierarchical graph model for conflict resolution with application to water diversion conflicts in China. INFOR: Inf. Syst. Oper. Res. **51**(3), 103–119 (2013)
21. Xu, H., Hipel, K.W., Kilgour, D.M.: Matrix representation of conflicts with two decision-makers. In: Procedings IEEE Inernational Conference System Man Cybern., vol. 1, pp. 1764–1769 (2007)
22. Xu, H., Hipel, K.W., Kilgour, D.M.: Matrix representation of solution concepts in multiple-decision-maker graph models. IEEE Trans. Syst. Man Cybern. **39**(1), 96–108 (2009)

Timing and Decision Making

Gil Greenstein$^{(\boxtimes)}$

Faculty of Technology Management, Holon Institute of Technology,
Holon, Israel
gilgr@hit.ac.il

Abstract. The paper presents a normative model which accounts for timing aspects of decision making under uncertainty. We build a model for a decision making process and then solve it, seeking the best timing to make a decision. It is based on several assumptions: information resources become more accurate over time (due to systematic improvements of a given information system), the value of utility or payoff functions deteriorates over time (moreover, loss of opportunities over time is also analyzed), and decision makers observe information only once, before making a decision. In addition, the assumptions of Bounded Rationality are integrated in the model, that is, decision makers stick to a rigid decision rule. The proposed analytical framework allows examining a decision rule over time. A cost of information gathering and a cost of decision delays are also incorporated in the model.

Keywords: Decision theory and analysis · Decision support systems · Implementation of DSS · Information economics

1 Introduction

In the modern era of information explosion, volumes of data should been processed to information and then later transformed to knowledge. In fact, we can collect data, process it to information and transform it to knowledge almost without limitations. The major question concerns to the scope of investment in those processes. Thus, the analysis of decision situations setting the best time to make a decision becomes essential. The best decision timing depends on several factors like amount of information and time needed to gather it, costs of information gathering as a function of time needed to process it, changes in a space of opportunities along the time and so on.

Adopting information technology allows to leverage the performance gradually. The paper accounts for changes in the value of information, which becomes more accurate, over time. Even assuming that a decision maker sticks with a given decision rule, that is not the optimal one, the paper shows that she still get an increasing (or at least non-decreasing) value of information over time. The adoption of a decision rule over time was discussed by Ahituv [1]. He identified the need to analyze a rigid decision rule in a decision-making process, which prevent to take an optimal decision, since a decision maker sticks with a current decision rule. Inability of a decision maker to react instantly to changes in the decision environment has been described from some points of view of Bounded Rationality [16, 17], and inability to react to changes [1]. In contrast, this is paper analyzes a scenario in which decision parameters are varied.

© Springer International Publishing Switzerland 2015
I. Linden et al. (Eds.): EWG-DSS 2014, LNBIP 221, pp. 89–100, 2015.
DOI: 10.1007/978-3-319-21536-5_8

This paper develops an analytical model of decision making over time. It incorporates several issues like systematic improvement of systems, use of more accurate information over time, loss of opportunities over time, cost of information gathering, and cost of decision delay. Section 2 reviews the literature on the Information Structure Model and the Blackwell Theorem [14]. It also describes the systematic informativeness ratio between two information systems [5], and demonstrates its possible implication on DSS implementation process. Section 3 presents the model and Sect. 4 applies it using a specific example. The last section concludes.

2   The Basic Models

2.1   The Information Structure Model and Blackwell Theorem

The basic model employed in this paper is the Information Structure Model [13]. This is a general model for comparing and rank ordering information systems based on the assumptions of rational behavior. According to the Information Structure Model, the following four elements determine the expected value of information: a vector of a priori probabilities of states, an information structure, a decision matrix and a payoff matrix.

Let S be a finite set of n states of nature: $S = \{S_1,..,S_n\}$ and P be a vector of a priori probabilities for each of the states of nature: $P = (p_1,..,p_n)$.

The information structure is a stochastic (Markovian) matrix that transmits signals out of states of nature. Let Y be a finite set of n signals, $Y = \{Y_1,..,Y_m\}$. An *information structure* Q is defined such that its elements obtain values between 0 and 1, $Q: SxY \rightarrow [0,1]$, where $Q_{i,j}$ is the probability that a state of nature S_i displays a signal Y_j and $\sum_{j=1}^{m} Q_{ij} = 1$.

The decision matrix links signals with the decision set of a decision-maker. Let A be a finite set of k possible decisions, $A = \{A_1,..,A_k\}$ and D be a decision function. Similar to Q, D is a stochastic (Markovian) matrix, namely, it is assumed that the decision selected for a given signal is not necessarily always the same. That is, $D:Y x A \rightarrow [0,1]$.

The payoff matrix presents the quantitative compensation to a decision-maker resulting from the combination of a decision chosen and a given state of nature. Let U be a payoff function: $U:A x S \rightarrow \mathfrak{R}$ (a combination of a state of nature and a decision provides a fixed compensation that is a real number), where $U_{i,j}$ is the compensation obtained by a decision maker when she decides "Ai", while state of nature "S_j" occurs.

The Information Structure Model enables a comparison of information systems using a quantitative measurement reflecting their economic values. An information structure Q_1 is said to be more informative than an information structure Q_2 if the expected payoff of using Q_1 is not lower than the expected payoff of using Q_2. The expected payoff is trace($\Pi*Q*D*U$), where trace is an operator that sums the diagonal elements of a square matrix. The objective function for maximizing the expected compensation is $\underset{D}{Max}(trace(\Pi * Q * D * U))$. When the utility function is linear, that is, a decision-maker is of the type EMV [13], the linear programming algorithm may be applied to solve the problem, where the variables are the elements of the decision matrix D. It can be proved that at least one of the optimal solutions is in a form of a decision matrix whose elements are 0 or 1 (a pure decision rule) [1]. For numerical illustrations of the model, see [1, 2, 7]. Although, decision makers are not necessarily of the type EMV, this model enables us to deal with monetary decisions, where the expected payoff is calculated in order to maximize profits. In Sect. 4 of this paper such an example is demonstrated.

Given two information systems that deal with the same states of nature and are represented by the information structures Q_1 and Q_2, Q_1 is defined as generally more informative than Q_2 if the expected payoff it generates is not lower than that of Q_2 for any a priori probability vector and any payoff matrix.[1] The rank ordering is transitive.[2]

Over the years researchers have developed analytical models to implement the concept of the Information Structure Model in order to evaluate the value of information technologies. Ahituv [2] demonstrates the life cycle of decision support information system using the model. Ahituv and Elovici [3] evaluate the performances of distributed information systems. Elovici et al. [10] use this method to compare performances of Information Filtering Systems. Ahituv and Greenstein [4] use this model to assess issues of centralization vs. decentralization. Aronovich and Spiegler [7] apply this model in order to assess the effectiveness of data mining processes. Ahituv and Greenstein [5] analyze the value of information during an implementation process of DSS. Elovici and Braha [9] describe the knowledge extracting in order to gain profitability over time.

Moreover, the model has been expanded to evaluate the value of information in several aspects: The value of a second opinion [6]; the value of information in non-linear models of the Utility Theory [16]; a situation of a two-criterion utility function [15]; the value of awareness to not-knowing situations [11]. The model has been also implemented to evaluate the value of information in postal services empirically [8], and in analysis of Quality Control methods [12]. Nevertheless, none of them examines the trade-off between information accuracy improving over time and payoffs decreasing over time. This research suggests a new method in order to analyze such decision situations.

2.2   The Systematic Informativeness Ratio

Ahituv and Greenstein [5] define the systematic informativeness ratio. This ratio defines the ability to upgrade a decision support system without the awareness of a decision maker, as it is described in the following definitions.

---

[1] In terms of the Information Structure Model, if for every possible payoff matrix U, and for every a priori probability matrix $\Pi \ \underset{D}{Max}(trace(\prod *Q_1 * D * U)) \ \geq \ \underset{D}{Max}(trace(\prod *Q_2 * D * U))$, then Q_1 is generally more informative than Q_2, denoted by $Q_1 \geq Q_2$. The Blackwell Theorem states that Q_1 is generally more informative than Q_2 if and only if there is a Markovian (stochastic) matrix R such that $Q_1 * R = Q_2$, where R is termed the **garbling** matrix.

[2] It should be noted that the general informativeness ratio is a partial rank ordering of information structures. There is not necessarily rank order between any two information structures.

Definition 1. Let Q_1 and Q_2 be two information structures representing two information systems operating on the same set of states of nature $S = \{S_1,...,S_n\}$ and producing the same set of signals $Y = \{Y_1,...,Y_m\}$. Q_1 is defined *systematically more informativ* than Q_2, denoted as

$$Q_1 \underset{S}{\geq} Q_2 \tag{2.1}$$

if for any decision situation (irrespective of payoffs and a priori probabilities) Q_1 is more informative than Q_2 under an optimal decision rule of Q_2. In other words, if Q_1 is systematically more informative than Q_2, then for every decision situation there exists an optimal decision rule of the inferior information structure Q_2 that can be used with the superior information structure Q_1, and guarantees at least the optimal outcomes of using Q_2.

Definition 2. Let Q_1 and Q_2 be two information structures representing two information systems operating on the same set of states of nature $S = \{S_1,...,S_n\}$ and producing the same set of signals $Y = \{Y_1,...,Y_m\}$. Assume Q_1 is generally more informative than Q_2. A *smooth implementation* of Q_1 instead of Q_2 is defined if for any level of usage p $(0 \leq p \leq 1)$

$$p * Q_1 + (1-p) * Q_2 \geq Q_2. \tag{2.2}$$

That is, for any probabilistic level of usage of the superior information system Q_1, the mean of the expected payoffs (compensation) that decision-makers gain is not less than that achieved by using only the inferior information system. It justifies a smooth implementation of the superior information structure Q_1.

Ahituv and Greenstein [5] prove that both definitions that detailed in Eqs. (2.1) and (2.2), are identical:

$$Q_1 \underset{S}{\geq} Q_2 \Leftrightarrow \forall p, 0 \leq p \leq 1, \ p * Q_1 + (1-p) * Q_2 \geq Q_2 \tag{2.3}$$

Their model allows to demonstrate a normative framework of evolutional implementation process of DSS. Although, a normative ratio does not necessarily reflect the real processes of DSS implementation, its internal mechanism is better explicable. In the next section we use this ratio to represent a consistent process of DSS improvement, adding the time dimension.

3   The Model for Decision Over Time

3.1   Improvement of Informativeness Level by Collecting Information Over Time

First, we assume that the value of information increases systematically (consistently). Let Q_1 and Q_2 be two information structures operating on the same set of states of nature $S = \{S_1,...,S_n\}$, and producing the same set of signals $Y = \{Y_1,...,Y_m\}$ and $\forall p, \ 0 \leq p \leq 1, \ p * Q_1 + (1-p) * Q_2 \geq Q_2$.

We also assume that the value of information that increases consistently is time dependent. Let Qt be an information structure, which represents the transformation over time from Q_2 to Q_1, that is

$$Qt = p(t) * Q_1 + (1 - p(t)) * Q_2$$

and $\begin{cases} p(0) = 0 \\ p(t1) = 1 \\ t1 > t2 > t3 \geq 0 \Rightarrow 1 > p(t2) \geq p(t3) \geq 0, \\ t4 > t1 \Rightarrow p(t4) = 1 \end{cases}$

where $p(t)$ is a monotonic continuous function, and it has a second derivative, while $0 \leq t \leq t1$.

Now we derive the expected payoff that increases over time. Let V_2 be the expected payoff (or expected utility) of Q_2 under an optimal decision rule. Let V_1 be the expected payoff (or expected utility) of Q_1 under the same decision rule. Thus, the value of information over time is defined as follows: $V_1 > V_2$.

$$trace(\Pi * Q_1 * D_{Q2} * U) = V_1$$

$$trace(\Pi * Q_2 * D_{Q2} * U) = V_2$$

$$V_1 > V_2, \ \Delta V = V_1 - V_2 > 0$$

3.2   The Deterioration of Expected Payoff (or Utility) Over Time

Let $U(t)$ be the utility matrix. Thus, $u(t)$ is a monotonic derivable function which decreases over time.

$$U_{(t)} = u(t) * \begin{pmatrix} U_{1,1} & \cdots & U_{1,n} \\ & \cdot & \\ & \cdot & \\ & \cdot & \\ U_{k,1} & \cdots & U_{k,n} \end{pmatrix} = u(t) * U$$

3.3   The Cost of Collection of Information Over Time

Let $C(t)$ be the cost of information gathering over time. Thus, $C(t)$ is a monotonic (non-decreased) derivable function. We define a function, $f(t)$, that calculates a tradeoff between level of availability of information, $p(t)$, and expected payoff (or utility) over time, $u(t)$.

$$f(t) = p(t) * u(t). \tag{3.1}$$

Theorem 1 (the proof is in the appendix) sets the sufficient condition for a local maximum of the expected utility over time:

$$\frac{\partial f(t)}{\partial t} * \Delta V - \frac{\partial C(t)}{\partial t} = -\frac{\partial u(t)}{\partial t} * V_2 \tag{3.2}$$

$$\frac{\partial^2 u(t)}{(\partial t)^2} * V_2 + \frac{\partial^2 f(t)}{(\partial t)^2} * \Delta V - \frac{\partial^2 C(t)}{(\partial t)^2} < 0 \tag{3.3}$$

Analyzing the first derivative (Eq. 3.2), we obtain that the right-hand side of the equation represents the marginal decline of the guaranteed expected value of information over time. In fact, it is the value of information that could be achieved without collection of further information. This expected value decreases over time. Moreover, the left-hand side of the equation represents the marginal increase of expected value of information over time. This improvement is influenced by the change of profits and cost, and the expected value of information over time. It is assumed that this expected value will increase as much as we delay our decision. Hence, the implication of the equation is that the marginal cost of losing guaranteed profit is equal to the marginal profit from increasing the accuracy of information. Thus, it is a potential extremum. Since the second derivative is negative (Eq. 3.3), it is a local maximum. In the next section we apply the model using a numerical example.

4 An Example of Decision Over Time

A startup company intends to sell its knowledge to a hi-tech firm choosing one from four competing firms (firms A-D, which produce innovative products) in return for receiving its options. It is known that only one of those four firms will succeed, hence, the CEO and the CFO of the startup company should find out the winner, in order to achieve a maximal expected payoff. If they make the right choice, the case of success, the company gains an enormous payoff; otherwise, in the case of failure, the payoff will reduce significantly. Firms A - C agree to wait 200 days for the decision. But, firm D agrees to wait only 150 days.

The model presented in Sect. 3 suggests the following steps in the decision process: First, the decision situation is presented, including the a priori probabilities (see Table 1 (a)) for success for each company, and the four alternatives (see Table 1(b)):

Then, we suppose that Q_2 is an information system during the initial state, where Y_j $(j = 1,..,4)$ are its four signals (see Table 2):

Table 1. (a). States on nature and probabilities, (b). Alternatives

State of Nature	Success	Probability	Decision
S_1	Product of firm A	0.5	A_1 - receive options of Firm A
S_2	Product of firm B	0.2	A_2 - receive options of Firm B
S_3	Product of firm C	0.2	A_3 - receive options of Firm C
S_4	Product of firm D	0.1	A_4 - receive options of Firm D
	(a)		(b)

Table 2. Information system Q_2

Si /Yj	$Y_1 = A$	$Y_2 = B$	$Y_3 = C$	$Y_4 = D$
S_1 = Success of Product A	1	0	0	0
S_2 = Success of Product B	0.4	0.6	0	0
S_3 = Success of Product C	0.4	0	0.4	0.2
S_4 = Success of Product D	0.4	0	0	0.6

In the next step we describe the increase of the informativeness level over time. During days 1-100 the chance for perfect information (that is represented by the unity matrix, I) increases by 0.4 % every day. During days 101-200 the chance for perfect information (that is represented by I) increases by 0.6 % every day. Hence, the information structure over time will look as follows:

$$Q(t) = \frac{4t}{1000} * I + \left(1 - \frac{4t}{1000}\right) * Q_2$$

$$s.t. \quad 0 \le t \le 100$$

$$Q(t) = \left(\frac{400}{1000} + \frac{6*(t-100)}{1000}\right) * I + \left(1 - \frac{400}{1000} - \frac{6*(t-100)}{1000}\right) * Q_2$$

$$s.t. \quad 100 \le t \le 200$$

$$\Leftrightarrow$$

$$Q(t) = \left(\frac{6*t}{1000} - \frac{200}{1000}\right) * I + \left(\frac{1200}{1000} - \frac{6*t}{1000}\right) * Q_2 \quad \textit{Hence, it can be shown that,} \, Q_1 = Q_{(200)} = I$$

$$s.t. \quad 100 \le t \le 200$$

Since, the option to sell the knowledge to firm D is feasible during the first 150 days, there are two payoff matrices, presented as follows (see Table 3):

Table 3. The payoff matrices

	S_1	S_2	S_3	S_4
A_1	255	5	5	5
A_2	10	260	10	10
A_3	0	0	250	0
A_4	15	15	15	265

	S_1	S_2	S_3	S_4
A_1	255	5	5	5
A_2	10	260	10	10
A_3	0	0	250	0

U_0: t $\le$ 150 (Decision/State of nature) U_1: 150 < t $\le$ 200 (Decision/State of nature)

Now we examine the deterioration of expected payoff (or utility) over time. The level of options decreases by a ratio of 0.1 % in the first 120 days. Then it decreases by a ratio of 0.2 % in the next 80 days. As was mentioned a deal should be reached in the period of 200 days. The company can hire an external expert that uses the DSS. Since the decision will be made once there is a need to analyze a priori the best timing of making a decision. The expected payoff over time deteriorates as follows:

$$U_0 * e^{-0.001*t}$$
$$s.t. \quad 0 \le t \le 120$$
$$U_0 * e^{-0.002*t} * e^{-(0.001-0.002)*120} \Leftrightarrow U * e^{-0.002*t+0.12}$$
$$s.t. \quad 120 \le t \le 150$$
$$U_1 * e^{-0.002*t} * e^{-(0.001-0.002)*120} \Leftrightarrow U1 * e^{-0.002*t+0.12}$$
$$s.t. \quad 150 < t \le 200$$

Finally, we calculate the cost of information gathering over time. It costs 30,000 units of money during days 1-100 and 45,000 units of money during days 101-200. Hence,

$$C(t) = 0.03 * (t)$$
$$s.t. \quad 0 \le t \le 100$$

$$C(t) = 0.03 * 100 + 0.045 * (t - 100) = 0.045 * t - 1.5$$
$$s.t. \quad 100 \le t \le 200$$

Thus, the optimization problem of expected profits over time will look as follows:

$$\underset{D,t}{Max}\left\{ \left(trace\Pi * \left(\frac{4t}{1000} * I + \left(1 - \frac{4t}{1000}\right) * Q_2 \right) * D * U * e^{-0.001*t} \right) - 0.03 * t \right\}$$
$$s.t. \quad 0 \le t \le 100$$

$$\underset{D,t}{Max}\left\{ \left[trace\Pi * \left(\frac{6*t}{1000} - 0.2 \right) * I + \left(1.2 - \frac{6*t}{1000}\right) * Q_2 * D * U * e^{-0.001*t} \right] - (0.045 * t - 1.5) \right\}$$
$$s.t. \quad 100 \le t \le 120$$

$$\underset{D,t}{Max}\left\{ \left[trace\Pi * \left(\frac{6*t}{1000} - 0.2 \right) * I + \left(1.2 - \frac{6*t}{1000}\right) * Q_2 * D * U * e^{-0.002*t+0.12} \right] - (0.045 * t - 1.5) \right\}$$
$$s.t. \quad 120 \le t \le 150$$

$$\underset{D,t}{Max}\left\{ \left[trace\Pi * \left(\frac{6*t}{1000} - 0.2 \right) * I + \left(1.2 - \frac{6*t}{1000}\right) * Q_2 * D * U_1 * e^{-0.002*t+0.12} \right] - (0.045 * t - 1.5) \right\}$$
$$s.t. \quad 150 < t \le 200$$

This problem is solved and the expected payoffs over time are calculated (see Table 4 and Fig. 1 for the first days 1 − 150).

Figure 1 shows that the expected profit is maximal when t = 120. If we have to decide in the first 100 days, the 63th day is the preferred day to make a decision, since

Table 4. Expected payoff over time during investigated points on time scale

The optimal decision rule		Expected payoff	Timing of decision making
Decision Rule	**Given Signal**	196.2	t=0
A1 - receive options of Firm A	**Y1 - A**	196.5759	t=62.14
A2 - receive options of Firm B	**Y2 - B**	196.4583	t=100
A3 - receive options of Firm C	**Y3 - C**	198.1345	t=120
A4 - receive options of Firm D	**Y4 – D**		
Decision Rule	**Given Signal**	194.4593	t=150
A1 - receive options of Firm A	Y1 - A	168.5398	t=200
A2 - receive options of Firm B	Y2 - B		
A3 - receive options of Firm C	Y3 - C		
A3 - receive options of Firm C	Y4 – D		

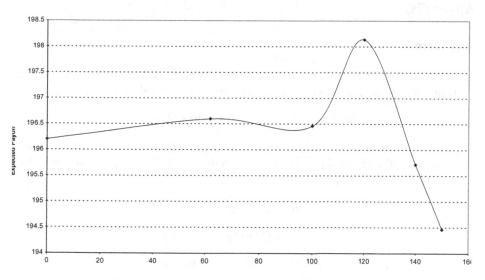

Fig. 1. Expected payoff over time during days 1-150

there is a local maximum in the 63th day. The impact of the rate of information gathering on the expected payoff can be shown by a severe increase of expected payoff between days 100 − 120, since the rate of collection of information increases. From day 120, the impact of the marginal cost of collection of information on timing of decision making is shown by a decrease of the expected value of information. After day 150 and till day 200, there is a significant decrease, since one alternative (A4 - receive options of Firm D) no longer exists.

5   Conclusions

This paper contributes to better understanding of decision processes over time, by adding the time dimension to design processes of DSS. It provides the cost benefits analysis of DSS. The example demonstrates how to calculate the various aspects of timing: level of information accuracy, cost of decision delays, and cost of gathering information over time. Being normative and generic, the proposed model is applicable not only for different situations in which the decision on decision timing should be made a priori, but for a wider spectrum of decision situations like dynamic decisions and reversible decisions. Thus, further research may extend the model and apply it to a dynamic decision environment in which an option not to decide a-priory on decision timing exists (a case dependent decision environment) and to situations in which a decision is reversible.

Appendix:

Theorem 1

1. Let Q_1 and Q_2 be two information structures operating on the same set of states of nature $S = \{S_1,...,S_n\}$, and producing the same set of signals $Y = \{Y_1,...,Y_m\}$.

$$\forall p, 0 \leq p \leq 1, \; p * Q_1 + (1-p) * Q_2 \geq Q_2$$

2. Let V_2 the expected payoff (or expected utility) of Q_2 under an optimal decision rule. Let V_1 the expected payoff (or expected utility) of Q_1 of V_2, by using the same given decision rule, $V_1 > V_2$

$$trace(\Pi * Q_1 * D_{Q2} * U) = V_1$$

$$trace(\Pi * Q_2 * D_{Q2} * U) = V_2$$

$$V_1 > V_2, \quad \Delta V = V_1 - V_2 > 0$$

3. Let Qt an information structure, which represent the transformation over time from Q_2 to Q_1.

$$Q_t = p(t) * Q_1 + (1 - p(t)) * Q_2$$

$$\begin{cases} p(0) = 0 \\ p(t1) = 1 \\ t1 > t2 > t3 \geq 0 \Rightarrow 1 > p(t2) \geq p(t3) \geq 0, \\ t4 > t1 \Rightarrow p(t4) = 1 \end{cases}$$

$p(t)$ is a monotonic Continuous function with a second derivative in the range $0 \le t \le t1$.

4. Let $U(t)$ the utility matrix, which differs over time

$$U_{(t)} = u(t)^* \begin{pmatrix} U_{1,1} & \cdots & U_{1,n} \\ & \cdot & \\ & \cdot & \\ & \cdot & \\ U_{k,1} & \cdots & U_{k,n} \end{pmatrix} = u(t) * U$$

5. Let $f(t)$, a function that calculates a tradeoff between availability and outcomes over time. $f(t) = p(t) * u(t)$
6. Let $C(t)$ the cost of collection of information over time. $C(t)$ is a monotonic (non-decreased) derivative function over time.

Hence, a sufficient condition for a local maximum of expected utility over time is:

i. $\frac{\partial f(t)}{\partial t} * \Delta V - \frac{\partial C(t)}{\partial t} = -\frac{\partial u(t)}{\partial t} * V_2$

ii. $\frac{\partial^2 u(t)}{(\partial t)^2} * V_2 + \frac{\partial^2 f(t)}{(\partial t)^2} * \Delta V - \frac{\partial^2 C(t)}{(\partial t)^2} < 0$

Proof:

(1) $trace(\Pi * Q_t * D_{Q2} * U(t)) =$
(2) $= trace(\Pi * (p(t) * Q_1 + (1 - p(t)) * Q_2) * D_{Q2} * U(t)) =$
(3) $= p(t) * trace(\Pi * Q_1 * D_{Q2} * u(t) * U) + (1 - p(t)) * trace(\Pi * Q_2 * D_{Q2} * u(t) * U) =$
(4) $= p(t) * u(t) * trace(\Pi * Q_1 * D_{Q2} * U) + (1 - p(t)) * u(t) * trace(\Pi * Q_2 * D_{Q2} * U)$
(5) It is given that

$$trace(\Pi * Q_1 * D_{Q2} * U) = V_1$$

$$trace(\Pi * Q_2 * D_{Q2} * U) = V_2$$

(6) Hence

$$p(t) * u(t) * trace(\Pi * Q_1 * D_{Q2} * U) + (1 - p(t)) * u(t) * trace(\Pi * Q_2 * D_{Q2} * u(t) * U) =$$

$$= p(t) * u(t) * V_1 + (1 - p(t)) * u(t) * V_2$$

(7) $= p(t) * u(t) * (V_1 - V_2) + u(t) * V_2 = f(t) * \Delta V + u(t) * V_2$
(8) A necessary condition for existence of a local extremum is that the first degree derivative is 0:

$$\frac{\partial}{\partial t}[(trace(\Pi * Q_t * D_{Q2} * U(t))) - C(t)] = 0$$

Thus: $\frac{\partial u(t)}{\partial t} * V_2 + \frac{\partial f(t)}{\partial t} * \Delta V - \frac{\partial C(t)}{\partial t} = 0$

(9) $\frac{\partial f(t)}{\partial t} * \Delta V - \frac{\partial C(t)}{\partial t} = - \frac{\partial u(t)}{\partial t} * V_2$

(10) A sufficient condition for a local maximum is that the second degree derivative is negative, hence: $\frac{\partial^2 u(t)}{(\partial t)^2} * V_2 + \frac{\partial^2 f(t)}{(\partial t)^2} * \Delta V - \frac{\partial^2 C(t)}{(\partial t)^2} < 0$

Q.E.D

References

1. Ahituv, N.: A comparison of information structure for a "rigid decision rule" case. Decis. Sci. **12**(3), 399–416 (1981)
2. Ahituv, N.: Describing the information system life cycle as an adjustment process between information and decisions. Int. J. Policy Anal. Inf. Syst. **6**(2), 133–145 (1982)
3. Ahituv, N., Elovici, Y.: Evaluating the performance of an application running on a distributed system. J. Oper. Res. Soc. **52**, 916–927 (2001)
4. Ahituv, N., Greenstein, G.: Systems inaccessibility and the productivity paradox. EJOR **161**, 505–524 (2005)
5. Ahituv, N., Greenstein, G.: Evolution or revolution of organizational information technology - modeling decision makers' perspective. JSSM **3**(1), 51–66 (2010)
6. Ahituv, N., Ronen, B.: Orthogonal information structure - a model to evaluate the information provided by a second opinion. Decis. Sci. **19**(2), 255–268 (1988)
7. Aronovich, L., Spiegler, I.: CM-tree: a dynamic clustered index for similarity search in metric databases. Data Knowl. Eng. **3**, 919–946 (2007)
8. Carmi, N., Ronen, B.: An empirical application of the information-structures model: the postal authority case. EJOR **92**, 615–627 (1996)
9. Elovici, Y., Braha, D.: A decision theoretic approach to data mining. IEEE Trans. **33**(1), 42–51 (2003)
10. Elovici, Y., Shapira, B., Kantor, P.B.: Using the information structure model to compare profile-based information filtering. Inf. Retrieval **6**(1), 75–97 (2003)
11. Greenstein, G., Ahituv, N.: The value of knowing that you do not know. Serdica J. Comput. **3**(2), 205–226 (2009)
12. Margaliot, N.: Selecting a quality control attribute sample: an information-economics method. Ann. Oper. Res. **91**, 83–104 (1999)
13. Marschak, J.: Economic of information systems. J. Am. Stat. Assoc. **66**, 192–219 (1971)
14. McGuire, C.B., Radner, R.: Decision and Organization, 2nd edn. University of Minnesota Press, Minneapolis (1986)
15. Ronen, B.: An information-economics approach to quality control attribute sampling. EJOR **73**, 430–442 (1994)
16. Rubinstein, A.: Modeling Bounded Rationality. MIT Press, Cambridge (1998)
17. Simon, H.A.: The New Science of Management Decisions. Harper and Row, New-York (1960)

Author Index

Printed in the United States
by Baker & Taylor Publisher Ser...

Printed in the United States
by Baker & Taylor Publisher Services